GRADE 3

STAAR Mathematics

PRACTICE

Table of Contents

Using This Book

What Is the STAAR Mathematics Assessment?

The State of Texas Assessments of Academic Readiness (STAAR) is the current assessment for students in the state of Texas. STAAR Mathematics assesses what students are expected to learn at each grade level according to the developmentally appropriate academic readiness and supporting standards outlined in the Texas Essential Knowledge and Skills (TEKS).

How Does This Book Help My Student(s)?

If your student is taking the STAAR Assessment for Mathematics, then as a teacher and/or parent you can use the mini-lessons, math practice pages and practice tests in this book to prepare for the STAAR Mathematics exam. This book is appropriate for on-grade-level students.

STAAR Mathematics Practice provides:

- Mini-lessons for assessed Math TEKS skills and strategies
- Word problems for assessed Math TEKS skills and strategies
- Questions for griddable and multiple-choice answer format
- Opportunities to familiarize students with STAAR format and question stems

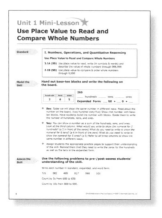

Introduce STAAR-aligned math concept, skill, or strategy

Practice with STAAR-aligned problems

Assess concepts, skills, and strategies with word problems

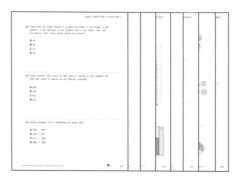

Simulate test-taking with full-length practice tests

STAAR Mathematics Practice/Assessed TEKS Alignme[nt]

I. Number, Operations, and Quantitative Reasoning	3.1	3.2	3.3	3.4	3.5	3.6	3.7	3.8	3.9	3.	3.	3.	3	3 3
Unit 1: Use Place Value to Read and Compare Whole Numbers	✔													✔
Unit 2: Use Place Value to Round Whole Numbers					✔									✔
Unit 3: Count Coins and Bills	✔													✔
Unit 4: Understand Fractions		✔												✔
Unit 5: Estimate Sums and Differences					✔									✔
Unit 6: Add Whole Numbers			✔											✔
Unit 7: Subtract Whole Numbers			✔											✔
Unit 8: Solve Two-Step Word Problems			✔											✔
Unit 9: Meaning of Multiplication				✔										✔
Unit 10: Properties of Multiplication				✔										✔
Unit 11: Multiply by Multiples of Ten				✔										✔
Unit 12: Solve Multiplication Problems				✔										✔
Unit 13: Meaning of Division				✔										

II. Patterns, Relationships, and Algebraic Reasoning	3.1	3.2	3.3	3.4	3.5	3.6	3.7	3.8	3.9	3.10	3.11	3.12	3.13	3.14 – 3.16
Unit 14: Identify and Extend Patterns						✔								✔
Unit 15: Patterns in Multiplication						✔								✔
Unit 16: Fact Families for Multiplication and Division						✔								✔
Unit 17: Patterns in Tables and Charts							✔							✔

III. Geometry and Spatial Reasoning	3.1	3.2	3.3	3.4	3.5	3.6	3.7	3.8	3.9	3.10	3.11	3.12	3.13	3.14 – 3.16
Unit 18: Describe and Compare Plane Figures								✔						
Unit 19: Describe and Compare Solid Figures								✔						✔
Unit 20: Identify Congruent Figures									✔					✔
Unit 21: Identify Lines of Symmetry									✔					✔
Unit 22: Numbers on a Number Line										✔				✔

IV. Measurement	3.1	3.2	3.3	3.4	3.5	3.6	3.7	3.8	3.9	3.10	3.11	3.12	3.13	3.14 – 3.16
Unit 23: Measure Length to the Nearest Quarter Inch											✔			✔
Unit 24: Find Perimeter											✔			✔
Unit 25: Understand Area											✔			✔
Unit 26: Measure Temperature												✔		✔
Unit 27: Time to the Minute												✔		✔

V. Probability and Statistics	3.1	3.2	3.3	3.4	3.5	3.6	3.7	3.8	3.9	3.10	3.11	3.12	3.13	3.14 – 3.16
Unit 28: Make a Pictograph													✔	✔
Unit 29: Make a Bar Graph													✔	✔
Unit 30: More Likely, Less Likely, Equally Likely													✔	✔

Unit 1 Mini-Lesson
Use Place Value to Read and Compare Whole Numbers

Standard

I. Number, Operations, and Quantitative Reasoning

Use Place Value to Read and Compare Whole Numbers

3.1A (SS) Use place value to read, write (in symbols and words) and describe the value of whole numbers through 999,999.

3.1B (SS) Use place value to compare and order whole numbers through 9,999.

Model the Skill

Hand out base-ten blocks and write the following on the board.

hundreds	tens	ones
2	6	5

265

_____ hundreds _____ tens _____ ones

Expanded Form: ___ 00 + ___ 0 + ___

◆ **Say:** *Today we will show the same number in different ways.* Read aloud the number on the board. (two hundred sixty-five) Show that number with base-ten blocks. Have students build the number with blocks. Guide them to write the number of hundreds, tens, and ones.

◆ **Say:** *You can show a number as a sum of the hundreds, tens, and ones. Look at the third column. What would you write to show the numeral for 2 hundreds?* (a 2 in front of the zeros) *What do you need to write to show the numeral for 6 tens?* (a 6 in front of the zero) *What do you need to write to show the numeral for 5 ones?* (a 5) Refer to all three columns to show the same number in different ways.

◆ Assign students the appropriate practice pages to support their understanding of the skill. Remind them that they need to write the zeros for the hundreds as well as the tens in the expanded form.

Assess the Skill

Use the following problems to pre-/post-assess students' understanding of the skill.

Write each number in standard, expanded, and word form.

721   582   490   817   968   101

Count by 5s from 600 to 650.

Count by 10s from 800 to 900.

Name _____ **Date** _____

Write the number shown in three different ways. Use base-ten blocks if you wish.

 ❶

hundreds	tens	ones
1	9	0

standard form: _____

expanded form: _____00 + _____0 + _____

word form: _____

❷ standard form: **249**   expanded form: _____ + _____ + _____

word form: _____

❸ standard form: _____   expanded form: **600 + 20 + 8**

word form: _____

❹ standard form: _____   expanded form: _____ + _____ + _____

word form: **eight hundred thirty-four**

❺ **Skip count by 100s.**

300 400 500 ___ ___ ___ ___

❻ **Skip count by 10s.**

460 470 480 ___ ___ ___ ___

❼ **Skip count by 5s.**

510 515 520 ___ ___ ___ ___

❽ **Look for a skip-counting pattern. Write the missing numbers.**

630, 640, 650, _____, _____, _____

☆ **Tell how you know the different ways to write a number.**

Name _____ Date _____

Fill in the blanks for each problem.

1 standard form: **732** expanded form: _____ + _____ + _____

word form: _____

2 standard form: _____ expanded form: **500 + 90 + 4**

word form: _____

3 standard form: _____ expanded form: _____ + _____ + _____

word form: **six hundred nine**

4 standard form: **813** expanded form: _____ + _____ + _____

word form: _____

Look for a skip-counting pattern. Write the missing numbers.

5
325, 330, 335, _____, _____, _____

6
500, 600, 700, _____, _____, _____

7
740, 750, 760, _____, _____, _____

8
445, 450, 455, _____, _____, _____

9
450, 550, 650, _____, _____, _____

10
975, 980, 985, _____, _____, _____

☆ **Tell how you know which number comes next.**

Name _____ Date _____

Write the number in the missing forms.

1 standard form: **768**

expanded form: _____

word form: _____

2 standard form: _____

expanded form: _____

word form: **four hundred seventy**

Look for a skip-counting pattern. Write the missing numbers.

3 630, 640, 650, _____, _____, _____

4 260, 270, 280, _____, _____, _____

5 945, 950, 955, _____, _____, _____

6 705, 710, 715, _____, _____, _____

7 420, 430, 440, _____, _____, _____

8 685, 690, 695, _____, _____, _____

9 825, 830, 835, _____, _____, _____

10 320, 330, 340, _____, _____, _____

Choose the correct answer for each problem.

11 Look at the pattern below. What number comes next?
805, 810, 815, _____

A 825

B 816

C 915

D 820

12 Look at the pattern below. What number comes next?
780, 790, 800, _____

A 880

B 810

C 801

D 900

Unit 2 Mini-Lesson

Use Place Value to Round Whole Numbers

Standard

> ## I. Number, Operations, and Quantitative Reasoning
>
> **Use Place Value to Round Whole Numbers**
>
> **3.5A (SS)** Round whole numbers to the nearest ten or hundred to approximate reasonable results in problem situations.

Model the Skill

Draw the following number line on the board.

Ask: How can you use a number line to help you round numbers? Look at the number 42. (Locate the number on the line and see which ten it is closer to.) Invite students to circle 42 on the number line and determine which ten it is closer to. (40)

Say: You can also round numbers to the nearest ten by looking at the ones digits. Ask: What digit is in the ones place of 42? (2) How does that help you round 42? (If the digit is less than 5, the tens digit stays the same. If it is 5 or greater, the tens digit increases by one.)

Assign students the appropriate practice page(s) to support their understanding of the skill.

Assess the Skill

Use the following problems to pre-/post-assess students' understanding of the skill. Have students round each number to the nearest ten and hundred.

| 75 | 145 | 213 | 382 | 161 | 758 |

Name _____ Date _____

Round each number to the nearest ten.

❶ 63 ➜ _____

❷ 623 ➜ _____

❸ 255 ➜ _____

❹ 403 ➜ _____

❺ 527 ➜ _____

Round each number to the nearest hundred.

❻ 419 ➜ _____

❼ 843 ➜ _____

❽ 309 ➜ _____

❾ 649 ➜ _____

❿ 950 ➜ _____

☆ **Tell how you round numbers to the nearest hundred.**

Name _____ Date _____

Round each number to complete the chart.

	Whole number	Rounded to the nearest ten	Rounded to the nearest hundred
❶	313		
❷	769		
❸	453		
❹	921		
❺	686		
❻	67		
❼	629		
❽	106		
❾	554		
❿		250	200
⓫	938		900
⓬		470	

 Tell how you solved rows 10–12.

Name _____ Date _____

Solve.

1 Write three numbers that round to 30 when rounded to the nearest ten.

_____ _____ _____

2 Write three numbers that round to 100 when rounded to the nearest hundred.

_____ _____ _____

3 Write three numbers that round to 70 when rounded to the nearest ten.

_____ _____ _____

4 Write three numbers that round to 400 when rounded to the nearest hundred.

_____ _____ _____

Circle the letter for the correct answer.

5 What number can round to 760 when it rounds to the nearest ten and 800 when it rounds to the nearest hundred?

A 751

B 763

C 754

D 768

6 What number rounds to 500 when it rounds to the nearest ten and to the nearest hundred?

A 507

B 491

C 540

D 504

Unit 3 Mini-Lesson ★
Count Coins and Bills

Standard

I. Number, Operations, and Quantitative Reasoning

Count Coins and Bills

3.1C (SS) Determine the value of a collection of coins and bills.

3.14A Identify the mathematics in everyday situations.

Model the Skill

Show examples of several coins including pennies, nickels, dimes, and quarters.

◆ **Ask:** *What types of coins do I have here?* (quarters, dimes, nickels, and pennies) *What is the value of each coin?* (25 cents, 10 cents, 5 cents, and 1 cent) *What is one dime and three pennies?* (13 cents)

◆ Assign students the appropriate practice page(s) to support their understanding of the skill.

Assess the Skill

Use the following problems to pre-/post-assess students' understanding of the skill. Ask students to determine the value of each amount of money.

Name _____ **Date** _____

Write each amount. Use the ¢ symbol.

 ❶

_____

❷

_____

❸

_____

❹

_____

❺

_____

❻

_____

❼

_____

❽

_____

 Tell how you count three different kinds of coins.

Name _____ **Date** _____

Match each money to each tag.

1     $3.01

2     $1.26

3     $1.60

4     $0.65

5        $1.41

6     $0.40

7     $2.06

8     $0.41

 Tell how you count to find the total amount of money.

STAAR Mathematics Practice Grade 3 • ©2013 Newmark Learning, LLC

Name _____ **Date** _____

Solve.

1 You have two dimes, two nickels, and two pennies. What amount of money do you have?

2 Molly has two quarters, one dime, and one nickel. How much money does Molly have?

Choose the correct answer for each problem.

3 You have two one-dollar bills, a nickel, and two pennies. What amount of money do you have?

    A $1.52

    B $2.52

    C $1.07

    D $2.07

4 You have one one-dollar bill, three dimes, and five pennies. What amount of money do you have?

    A $1.35

    B $1.45

    C $1.08

    D $1.53

Unit 4 Mini-Lesson ★
Understand Fractions

Standard

I. Number, Operations, and Quantitative Reasoning

Understand Fractions

3.2C (RS) Use fraction names and symbols to describe fractional parts of whole objects or sets of objects (denominators of 12 or less).

Model the Skill

Draw the following figure on the board.

- ◆ **Say:** *Today we are going to learn about fractions. A fraction names part of a whole or part of a group. Look at this rectangle. How many equal parts is the rectangle divided into?* (2) *Each part is one-half of the whole rectangle.*

- ◆ Write the fraction $\frac{1}{2}$ on the board. Have students look at the fraction $\frac{1}{2}$ and point to the numerator. **Say:** *The numerator is the top number of a fraction. The numerator names a part of the whole.* Have students point to the denominator. **Say:** *The denominator is the bottom number of a fraction. The denominator tells how many equal parts are in the whole.*

- ◆ Model writing the fraction for the rectangle again. **Ask:** *How many equal parts are in the whole rectangle?* (2) *What fraction names each equal share or part?* ($\frac{1}{2}$) Have students practice writing the fraction for similar shapes sectioned in halves, thirds, and fourths or quarters.

- ◆ Assign students the appropriate practice page(s) to support their understanding of the skill and share their strategies for finding the missing numbers in each fraction. They should recognize that the denominator is always the same as the number of equal parts. Have them identify whether the numerator or the denominator is the missing number.

Assess the Skill

Use the following problems to pre-/post-assess students' understanding of the skill.

- ◆ **Ask:** *How many equal parts are in the whole? How many equal parts are shaded? What fraction shows the shaded part?*

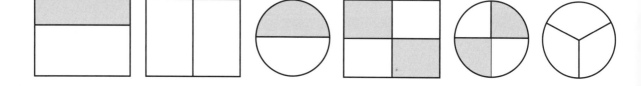

Name _____ Date _____

Match the picture with the fraction that names the shaded part.

1
$\dfrac{1}{2}$

2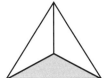
$\dfrac{1}{8}$

3
$\dfrac{2}{8}$

4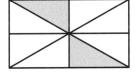
$\dfrac{1}{3}$

5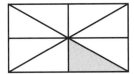
$\dfrac{1}{2}$

6
$\dfrac{1}{4}$

7
$\dfrac{2}{4}$

8
$\dfrac{2}{3}$

 Tell how you made each match.

Name _____ **Date** _____

Write the missing numbers.

1 4 equal parts

$\dfrac{\boxed{}}{4}$ is shaded.

2 6 equal parts

$\dfrac{\boxed{}}{6}$ is shaded.

3 _____ equal parts

$\dfrac{\boxed{}}{\boxed{}}$ is shaded.

4 _____ equal parts

$\dfrac{\boxed{}}{\boxed{}}$ is shaded.

5 4 equal parts

$\dfrac{\boxed{}}{4}$ is shaded.

6 6 equal parts

$\dfrac{\boxed{}}{6}$ is shaded.

7 _____ equal parts

$\dfrac{\boxed{}}{\boxed{}}$ is shaded.

8 _____ equal parts

$\dfrac{\boxed{}}{\boxed{}}$ is shaded.

☆ **Tell how you found the missing numbers.**

STAAR Mathematics Practice Grade 3 • ©2013 Newmark Learning, LLC

Name _____ **Date** _____

Solve.

1 We cut the grapefruit in 2 equal pieces. I ate 1 piece. How much did I eat?

2 We have 3 kittens. 2 kittens have stripes and 1 kitten has spots. What fraction of the kittens has spots?

3 Sloane has 4 cards in her hand. 3 cards are red. The rest are black. What fraction of the cards is red?

4 A pizza has 8 slices. 3 slices have olives. What fraction of the pizza has olives?

Circle the letter for the correct answer.

5 The book has 8 pages. 5 pages have pictures. What fraction of the book's pages has pictures?

A $\frac{1}{8}$

B $\frac{1}{5}$

C $\frac{8}{5}$

D $\frac{5}{8}$

6 Austin's room has 3 lights. 2 of the lights are on. 1 of the lights is off. What fraction of the lights in Austin's room is on?

A $\frac{1}{2}$

B $\frac{1}{3}$

C $\frac{2}{2}$

D $\frac{2}{3}$

Unit 5 Mini-Lesson ★
Estimate Sums and Differences

Standard

I. Number, Operations, and Quantitative Reasoning

Estimate Sums and Differences

3.5B (SS) Use strategies including rounding and compatible numbers to estimate solutions to addition and subtraction problems.

Model the Skill

Write the following problem on the board.

$$27 + 42 =$$

◆ **Say:** *Today we are going to estimate sums and differences. A sum is the total when you add. A difference is the amount that is left when you subtract. Look at this problem. Will you round the addends to the nearest ten or nearest hundred? Why?* (Answer: ten, because the addends are much less than 100)

◆ **Ask:** *How can you use rounding to estimate the sum of 27 and 42?* (Round 27 to 30 and 42 to 40. Then add 30 and 40 to get 70.) *Why might rounding numbers to the nearest ten make it easier to add?* (Possible answer: It is easy to add tens.)

◆ Assign students the appropriate practice page(s) to support their understanding of the skill.

Assess the Skill

Use the following problems to pre-/post-assess students' understanding of the skill. Have students round each addend to the nearest ten or hundred and then find the sum or difference.

65	85	315	465	841
+ 27	− 17	+ 178	− 189	− 96

Name _____ Date _____

Round each number to the nearest ten. Then estimate the sum or difference.

1
302 → ☐
+ 204 → + ☐

2
192→ ☐
– 95 → – ☐

3
681→ ☐
– 217→ – ☐

4
$$\begin{array}{r} 323 \\ -\ 267 \end{array}$$

5
$$\begin{array}{r} 286 \\ +\ 579 \end{array}$$

6
$$\begin{array}{r} 764 \\ -\ 397 \end{array}$$

7
$$\begin{array}{r} 203 \\ +\ 373 \end{array}$$

8
$$\begin{array}{r} 452 \\ -\ 236 \end{array}$$

9
$$\begin{array}{r} 774 \\ +\ 189 \end{array}$$

10
$$\begin{array}{r} 406 \\ +\ 328 \end{array}$$

11
$$\begin{array}{r} 709 \\ -\ 166 \end{array}$$

12
$$\begin{array}{r} 227 \\ +\ 364 \end{array}$$

13
$$\begin{array}{r} 423 \\ -\ 171 \end{array}$$

14
$$\begin{array}{r} 89 \\ +\ 516 \end{array}$$

15
$$\begin{array}{r} 964 \\ -\ 108 \end{array}$$

 Tell how you estimated the sum for Problem 14.

Name _____ **Date** _____

Round each number to the nearest ten. Then estimate the sum or difference.

1   149
     + 318

2   452
     – 39

3   278
     + 337

4   488
     + 325

5   346
     – 175

6   227
     + 579

7   988
     – 269

8   764
     – 397

9   167
     + 153

10   308
     – 149

11   834
     + 109

12   414
     + 299

13   318
     + 423

14   781
     – 119

15   66
     + 385

16   207
     + 484

17   847
     – 175

18   389
     + 232

19   905
     – 368

20   613
     – 87

 Write how you estimated the sum for Problem 18.

Name _____ Date _____

Solve.

1 Eva has 183 beads. She uses 37 beads to make a necklace. About how many beads does she have left over?

_____ beads

2 Rory has 132 baseball cards in his collection. His grandfather gives him 175 more cards. About how many cards does he now have in his collection?

_____ baseball cards

3 Last week's groceries cost 134 dollars. This week's groceries cost 158 dollars. About how much did the groceries cost in all?

_____ dollars

4 Collette has 246 stickers. She gives 28 to her brother. About how many stickers does Collette have left?

_____ stickers

Circle the letter for the correct answer.

5 Which problem has a sum of about 800?

A 523 – 307

B 523 + 307

C 442 + 302

D 496 + 402

6 Which problem has a difference of about 70?

A 764 – 632

B 64 + 134

C 278 – 205

D 489 – 411

Unit 6 Mini-Lesson ★
Add Whole Numbers

Standard

I. Number, Operations, and Quantitative Reasoning

Add Whole Numbers

3.3A (SS) Model addition and subtraction using pictures, words, and numbers.

Model the Skill

Hand out base-ten blocks and write the following problem on the board.

$$\begin{array}{r} 42 \\ + \ 29 \\ \hline \end{array}$$

◆ **Say:** *We are going to add today. We are going to find the sum. A sum is the total amount. How many ones are there in all?* (11) Allow students to count or add the ones. Record the ones in the vertical addition.

◆ **Ask:** *How many tens are there in all?* (7) Record the tens. **Ask:** *What is the sum of 42 + 29?* (71) Help students connect the models to the standard algorithm by adding the ones first. Accept other ways to find the sum.

◆ **Ask:** *How did you find the answer? How many ones are there in all?* (11) *Did you have to regroup the ones?* (yes) *After you regrouped the ones into ten and one, how many tens are there in all?* (7) *What is the sum?* (71)

◆ Assign students the appropriate practice page(s) to support their understanding of the skill.

Assess the Skill

Use the following problems to pre-/post-assess students' understanding of the skill.

$$\begin{array}{r} 56 \\ + \ 39 \\ \hline \end{array} \qquad \begin{array}{r} 227 \\ + \ 168 \\ \hline \end{array} \qquad \begin{array}{r} 605 \\ + \ 128 \\ \hline \end{array} \qquad \begin{array}{r} 581 \\ + \ 234 \\ \hline \end{array}$$

Name _____ Date _____

Find the sum for each problem.

1   346

    + 122

hundreds	tens	ones
3	4	6
+ 1	2	2

2   226
   + 43

3   323
   + 44

4   681
   + 217

5   107
   + 16

6   151
   + 54

7   206
   + 98

8   314
   + 37

9   720
   + 81

10   476
   + 101

11   313 + 256

12   507 + 184

13   375 + 246

14   508 + 132

15   79 + 644

16   264 + 708

☆   **Tell how you know your answer is reasonable.**

Name _____ **Date** _____

Find the sum for each problem.

①   586
      + 13

②   204
      + 46

③   118
      + 343

④   600
      + 286

⑤ 245 + 132

⑥ 586 + 213

⑦ 421 + 369

⑧ 355 + 273

⑨ 300 + 675

⑩ 266 + 128

⑪ 73 + 643

⑫ 564 + 206

⑬ 546 + 216

⑭ 354 + 165

⑮ 67 + 812

⑯ 301 + 129

⑰ 392 + 135

⑱ 209 + 372

⑲ 272 + 437

⑳ 613 + 208

 Write the steps you follow to add multi-digit numbers.

Name _____ Date _____

Solve.

1 The lawn mower costs 329 dollars. The hedge clippers cost 178 dollars. How much do the tools cost in all?

2 Reeve scored 453 points the first time she played her new video game. She scored 518 points the second time she played. What is her combined score?

3 Sam has 373 craft sticks. He buys a box of 425 more craft sticks. How many sticks does Sam have in all?

4 Abby walks 146 yards to school from her house. The library is another 456 yards from school. What is the distance in yards from Abby's house to the library?

Circle the letter for the correct answer.

5 Helen needs 152 sequins for her costume. Freddie needs 209 sequins for his costume. How many sequins do they need in all?

A 361

B 351

C 461

D 261

6 Joanie has 387 pumpkin seeds. Harrison has 562 pumpkin seeds. How many pumpkin seeds do they have in all?

A 849

B 949

C 739

D 938

Unit 7 Mini-Lesson ★
Subtract Whole Numbers

Standard

I. Number, Operations, and Quantitative Reasoning

Subtract Whole Numbers

3.3A (SS) Model addition and subtraction using pictures, words, and numbers.

Model the Skill

Write the following problems on the board.

```
  57        65
- 26      - 17
```

◆ **Say:** *We are going to subtract today. We are going to find the difference. Look at the first problem on the board. How many ones are there in the number 57?* (7) *How many ones are you going to take away?* (6) Allow students to record the difference.

◆ **Ask:** *How many tens are there in 57?* (5) *How many tens are you going to take away?* (2) Allow students to record the remaining tens. (3) **Ask:** *What is the difference of 57 – 26?* (31)

◆ **Say:** *Look at the next problem. What happens when you subtract the ones?* Students should recognize that there are not enough ones to subtract and therefore they must regroup. Discuss how to regroup and record the regrouped ten. **Ask:** *How many ones and tens are left after subtracting?* (8 ones, 4 tens) *What is the difference?* (48)

◆ Assign students the appropriate practice page(s) to support their understanding of the skill.

Assess the Skill

Use the following problems to pre-/post-assess students' understanding of the skill.

```
   48          185          307          465
 - 29        - 118        - 126        - 346
```

Name _____ **Date** _____

Find the difference for each problem.

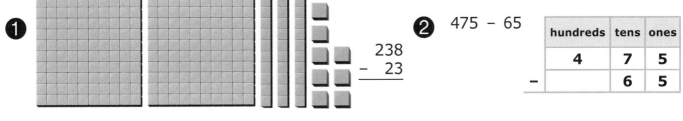

❶

238 – 23

```
  238
-  23
```

❷ 475 – 65

hundreds	tens	ones
4	7	5
−	6	5

❸
```
  187
-  51
```

❹
```
  409
- 108
```

❺
```
  246
- 125
```

❻
```
  641
- 322
```

❼
```
  341
- 221
```

❽
```
  352
- 307
```

❾
```
  427
-  64
```

❿
```
  754
- 383
```

⓫
```
  608
- 218
```

⓬ 321 – 30

⓭ 800 – 136

⓮ 784 – 365

 Tell how you know your answer is reasonable.

Name _____ **Date** _____

Find the difference for each problem.

1
```
   246
 - 122
```

2
```
   208
 -  46
```

3
```
   718
 - 343
```

4
```
   800
 - 278
```

5 354 – 165

6 680 – 645

7 409 – 73

8 549 – 256

9 421 – 369

10 392 – 128

11 783 – 674

12 586 – 213

13 437 – 206

14 354 – 272

15 861 – 812

16 992 – 875

17 400 – 204

18 909 – 372

19 772 – 437

20 613 – 318

 Write the steps you took to solve Problem 18.

Name _____ Date _____

Find the difference for each problem.

1 The lawn mower costs 329 dollars. The hedge clippers cost 178 dollars. How much more does the lawn mower cost?

2 Reeve scored 453 points the first time she played her new video game. She scored 618 points the second time she played. By how many points did her score improve the second time?

3 Sam has 875 craft sticks. He uses 798 sticks to build a model. How many sticks does Sam have left?

4 Abby walks 146 yards to school from her house. The park is 655 yards from her house. How much farther is the park from her house compared to the school?

Circle the letter for the correct answer.

5 Helen needs 152 sequins for her costume. Freddie needs 209 sequins for his costume. How many more sequins does Freddie need?

A 47

B 57

C 67

D 157

6 Joanie has 387 pumpkin seeds. Harrison has 562 pumpkin seeds. How many more pumpkin seeds does Harrison have?

A 225

B 185

C 285

D 175

Unit 8 Mini-Lesson
Solve Two-Step Word Problems

Standard

I. Number, Operations, and Quantitative Reasoning

Solve Two-Step Word Problems

3.3B (RS) Select addition or subtraction and use the operation to solve problems involving whole numbers through 999.

3.14B Solve problems that incorporate understanding the problem, making a plan, carrying out the plan, and evaluating the solution for reasonableness.

Model the Skill

Hand out counters and write the following problem on the board.

Sam has 3 apples and some bananas.
He has 8 pieces of fruit in all.
How many bananas does Sam have?

$3 + b = 8$

◆ **Say:** *Today we are going to solve problems that use a letter to stand for an unknown quantity. Look at this word problem. What do we know?* (Sam has 3 apples and some bananas. He has 8 pieces of fruit in all.) *What do we need to find out?* (how many bananas Sam has) *What letter should we use to represent the number of bananas?* (b) Point out that any letter can be used to represent an unknown quantity.

◆ Using red counters, model the apples. Ask a volunteer to add yellow counters to make a total of 8. **Ask:** *How many apples are there?* (3) *How many bananas did we add to make 8 pieces of fruit in all?* (5) *How many counters are there in all?* (8)

◆ Assign students the appropriate practice page(s) to support their understanding of the skill.

Assess the Skill

Use the following problems to pre-/post-assess students' understanding of the skill.

Lila has 6 strawberries. She eats 1. Then she gives 3 away. How many strawberries does she have left?

The orchard had 8 rows of apple trees. There were 7 trees in each row. 2 trees were cut down after they were damaged in a storm. How many trees are remaining in the orchard?

Name _____ **Date** _____

Write the missing numbers.

1 Lily bakes 8 muffins. She bakes 4 more. She gives 3 muffins to her friends. How many muffins (*m*) does she have now?

8 + 4 − 3 = *m*

8 + 4 − 3 = _____

m = _____

Lily has _____ muffins now.

2 Renee invites 14 guests to her party. Her mom invites 2 more guests. 5 people cannot come. How many guests (*g*) will be at the party?

14 + 2 − 5 = *g*

14 + 2 − 5 = _____

g = _____

There will be _____ guests at the party.

3 Ms. Green picked vegetables from her garden. She picked some tomatoes, 7 carrots, and 5 peppers. She picked 19 vegetables in all. How many tomatoes (*t*) did she pick?

Ms. Green picked _____ tomatoes.

4 Sophie had 17 apples. Mark had 15 apples. They used 8 apples to bake a pie. How many apples (*a*) do they have left?

They have _____ apples left.

5 Addie has 8 plates. José has twice as many plates as Addie.

How many plates does José have? _____

How many more plates does José have compared with Addie? _____

How many plates do they have in all? _____

 Tell how you solved Problem 2.

Name _____ **Date** _____

Solve.

1 Lucy had 18 apples. She gave 6 to Eric and some to Sue. She has 5 apples left. How many apples did she give to Sue?

n = _____

2 Sasha's baseball team played 16 games. The team won 9 games and tied 2 games. How many games did the team lose?

n = _____

3 Callie read 8 pages of a book on Monday. She read 9 pages on Tuesday. She read the rest of the book on Wednesday. There are 32 pages in the book. How many pages did she read on Wednesday?

n = _____

4 Fred has some blue pens. He has 9 black pens and 5 red pens. He has 25 pens in all. How many blue pens does he have?

n = _____

5 Joseph has 6 stickers. Rachel has three times as many stickers as Joseph.

How many stickers does Rachel have? _____

How many more stickers does Rachel have than Joseph? _____

How many stickers do they have in all? _____

6 Finbar has 67 craft sticks. Lindsay has 45 sticks. They will use 52 sticks to build a model.

How many more sticks does Finbar have? _____

What is the total number of craft sticks they have? _____

How many sticks will they have left after they build their model? _____

 Explain how you solved Problem 4.

Name _____ Date _____

**Write a number sentence to solve the problem.
Then solve the problem.**

1 There are 3 apples, 4 pears, and 6 bananas in a fruit bowl. How many pieces of fruit are in the bowl?

2 Kit has some green balloons, 6 yellow balloons, and 5 blue balloons. She has 20 balloons in all. How many green balloons (b) does she have?

3 Marie runs 11 miles in three days. She runs 3 miles on each of the first two days. How many miles does she run on the third day?

4 Evan baked 8 bran muffins and 7 blueberry muffins. He gave 3 of his muffins to a friend. How many muffins (m) does Evan have left?

Circle the letter for the correct answer.

5 There are 3 apple tarts and twice as many peach tarts. How many tarts are there in all?

A 9
B 8
C 6
D 5

6 Carla has 4 rows of rose bushes in her garden. Each row has 6 bushes. If she plants one more row of 6 bushes, how many rose bushes will she have?

A 10
B 16
C 24
D 30

Unit 9 Mini-Lesson ★
Meaning of Multiplication

Standard

I. Number, Operations, and Quantitative Reasoning

Meaning of Multiplication

3.4A (SS) Learn and apply multiplication facts through 12 x 12 using concrete models and objects.

3.4B (RS) Solve and record multiplication problems (up to two digits times one digit).

Model the Skill

Hand out counters.

◆ **Say:** *We are going to see how addition and multiplication are related.* Have students use counters to model 4 groups of 3.

◆ **Ask:** *How many equal groups do you have?* (4) *How many counters are there in each group?* (3) *How many counters are there in all?* (12)

◆ **Say:** *You can record 4 groups of 3 as an addition sentence or as a multiplication sentence.* Have students record the sum and the product. **Ask:** *What is the sum of 3 + 3 + 3 + 3?* (12) *What is the product of 4 x 3?* (12) *Remember, to multiply you need equal groups.*

◆ Assign students the appropriate practice page(s) to support their understanding of the skill.

Assess the Skill

Use the following problems to pre-/post-assess students' understanding of the skill.

$4 + 4 + 4 =$ _____

$3 \times 4 =$ _____

$6 + 6 =$ _____

$2 \times 6 =$ _____

STAAR Mathematics Practice Grade 3 • ©2013 Newmark Learning, LLC

Name _____ **Date** _____

Use counters to model the problem. Draw a picture to show your work. Complete each number sentence.

 4 groups of 3

3 + 3 + 3 + 3 = _____

4 x 3 = _____

 2 groups of 8

8 + 8 = _____

2 x 8 = _____

 3 groups of 5

5 + 5 + 5 = _____

3 x 5 = _____

 4 groups of 5

5 + 5 + 5 + 5 = _____

4 x 5 = _____

 6 groups of 2

2 + 2 + 2 + 2 + 2 + 2 = _____

6 x 2 = _____

 3 groups of 6

6 + 6 + 6 = _____

3 x 6 = _____

 Tell how both number sentences describe your picture.

Name _____ **Date** _____

Draw a picture for each multiplication sentence. Describe the picture. Then find the product.

 5 x 2 = _____

 4 x 5 = _____

_____

_____

_____

_____

 6 x 4 = _____

 8 x 2 = _____

_____

_____

_____

_____

 3 x 7 = _____

 4 x 9 = _____

_____

_____

_____

_____

☆ **Write about the steps you took to find the product.**

Name _____ **Date** _____

Solve.

1 There are 3 equal groups of apples. Each group has 5 apples. How many apples are there in all?

2 There are 4 bowls of plums. Each bowl has 3 plums. How many plums are there in all?

3 Erin runs 6 miles each day for 3 days. How many miles does she run in all? Write an addition sentence and a multiplication sentence that show the total.

4 There are 4 pans of muffins. Each pan has 6 muffins. How many muffins are there in all?

Circle the letter for the correct answer.

5 There are 5 trays of pies. Each tray has 4 pies. Which expression can be used to show the total number of pies?

A 4 + 5

B 4 + 4 + 4 + 4

C 5 × 4

D 5 × 5 × 5 × 5

6 There are 7 people fishing at the lake. Each person catches 3 fish. What is the total number of fish caught?

A 10

B 14

C 20

D 21

Unit 10 Mini-Lesson ★
Properties of Multiplication

Standard

I. Number, Operations, and Quantitative Reasoning

Properties of Multiplication

3.4A (SS) Learn and apply multiplication facts through 12 x 12 using concrete models and objects.

3.4B (RS) Solve and record multiplication problems (up to two digits times one digit).

Model the Skill

Hand out counters.

◆ Have students use counters to model the commutative property of multiplication. **Say:** *Today we are going to multiply two numbers and then change the order of the numbers to see if the product will change.* Have students model along as you demonstrate how to show 3 x 2 with counters.

◆ **Ask:** *How many groups of counters are there? How many counters are in each group? What is the product of 3 x 2?*

◆ **Say:** *Now let's see what happens to the product when we change the order of the numbers.* Guide students to model 2 x 3. **Ask:** *How many groups of counters are there? How many counters are there in each group? What is the product of 2 x 3? Does changing the order of the numbers change the product?* (no) *If you know 3 x 2 = 6, then you know 2 x 3 = 6.*

◆ Assign students the appropriate practice page(s) to support their understanding of the skill.

Assess the Skill

Use the following problems to pre-/post-assess students' understanding of the skill.

3 x 4 = _____   2 x (2 x 3) = _____

4 x 6 = _____   (2 x 2) x 3 = _____

5 x 7 = _____   4 x (2 x 2) = _____

8 x 8 = _____   (4 x 2) x 2 = _____

Name _____ **Date** _____

Use counters to model each problem.
Complete the number sentence for each problem.

4 x 2 = _____   2 x 4 = _____

4 x 6 = _____   6 x 4 = _____

 (2 x 2) x 4   2 x (2 x 4)

↓   ↓

_____ x 4 = _____   2 x _____ = _____

 (2 x 5) x 2   2 x (5 x 2)

10   x 2 = _____   2 x   10   = _____

 5 x 7   6 x 9

(5 x 3) + (5 x 4)   (6 x 5) + (6 x 4)

_____ + _____ = _____   _____ + _____ = _____

5 x 7 = _____   6 x 9 = _____

 4 x 8   3 x 7

(4 x 4) + (4 x 4)   (3 x 3) + (3 x 4)

_____ + _____ = _____   _____ + _____ = _____

4 x 8 = _____   3 x 7 = _____

 Pick three numbers. Tell about the product when the grouping is changed.

Name _____ **Date** _____

Write two true multiplication sentences for each model.

❷

_____

_____

_____

_____

Show two ways to solve each problem.

❸ 2 x 2 x 3

_____ x _____ = _____

_____ x _____ = _____

❹ 2 x 4 x 3

_____ x _____ = _____

_____ x _____ = _____

❺ 4 x 2 x 3

_____ x _____ = _____

_____ x _____ = _____

❻ 2 x 3 x 3

_____ x _____ = _____

_____ x _____ = _____

Fill in the missing number to find the product.

❼ 5 x 9

(5 x 5) + (5 x _____)

_____ + _____ = _____

5 x 9 = _____

❽ 2 x 9

(2 x _____) + (2 x 4)

_____ + _____ = _____

2 x 9 = _____

❾ 7 x 8

(7 x _____) + (7 x _____)

_____ + _____ = _____

7 x 8 = _____

❿ 8 x 9

(8 x _____) + (8 x _____)

_____ + _____ = _____

8 x 9 = _____

 Write about how you solved Problem 10.

Name _____ **Date** _____

Solve.

1 There are 8 rows of apple trees. Each row has 7 trees. Write two multiplication sentences that show the total number of apple trees.

2 There are 8 pots of corn. Each pot has 6 corncobs. Write two multiplication sentences to show the total number of corncobs.

3 There are 5 bags of beets. Each bag has 4 beets. Write two multiplication sentences to show the total number of beets.

4 There are 2 bakers. Each baker has 4 pans. Each pan has 6 cupcakes. Write 2 expressions that show the total number of cupcakes.

Circle the letter for the correct answer.

5 Which expression is equal to 4 x 8?

    A (4 x 5) + (4 x 3)

    B 8 x 4

    C (4 x 4) + (4 x 4)

    D all of the above

6 There are 2 buses. There are 7 girls and 3 boys on each bus. Which expression shows the total number of boys and girls on the buses?

    A 3 x (7 + 2)

    B 2 x (7 + 3)

    C (2 + 3) x 7

    D 2 + 3 + 7

Unit 11 Mini-Lesson ★
Multiply by Multiples of Ten

Standard

I. Number, Operations, and Quantitative Reasoning

Multiply by Multiples of Ten

3.4A (SS) Learn and apply multiplication facts through 12 x 12 using concrete models and objects.

3.4B (RS) Solve and record multiplication problems (up to two digits times one digit).

Model the Skill

Hand out ten-rods and write the following problems on the board.

$$1 \times 10 = 10 \qquad 1 \times 20 = 20$$
$$2 \times 10 = 20 \qquad 2 \times 20 = 40$$

◆ Have students use counters to model the first problem. **Say:** *Today we are going to look for patterns when we multiply by multiples of ten.* Demonstrate how to show 1 x 10 with base-ten blocks.

◆ **Ask:** *How many groups of tens are there? How many counters are there in the group? What is the product of 1 x 10?*

◆ **Say:** *Now let's try multiplying numbers by 20. What pattern do you see when we multiply with 20?* (Possible response: The product is the same as the fact in the tens place with a zero in the ones place.)

◆ Follow a similar process for multiplying 2 x 10 and 2 x 20.

◆ Assign students the appropriate practice page(s) to support their understanding of the skill.

Assess the Skill

Use the following problems to pre-/post-assess students' understanding of the skill.

1 x 20	2 x 20	3 x 20
4 x 20	5 x 20	6 x 20

STAAR Mathematics Practice Grade 3 • ©2013 Newmark Learning, LLC

Name _____ **Date** _____

Look for patterns. Then complete each fact.

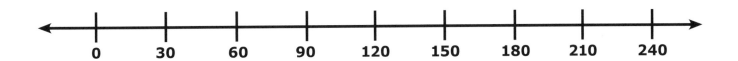

0   30   60   90   120   150   180   210   240

❶ 1 x 30 = _____

2 x 30 = _____

3 x 30 = _____

4 x 30 = _____

5 x 30 = _____

❷ 30 x 6 = _____

30 x 8 = _____

7 x 30 = _____

8 x 30 = _____

4 x 60 = _____

❸ 2 x 60 = _____

3 x 60 = _____

3 x 30 = _____

2 x 90 = _____

4 x 60 = _____

Use the number line. Find each product.

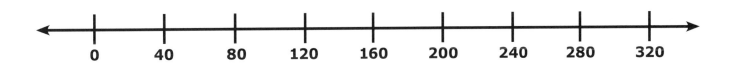

0   40   80   120   160   200   240   280   320

❹ 40 x 4 = _____

40 x 3 = _____

40 x 2 = _____

1 x 40 = _____

0 x 40 = _____

❺ 1 x 80 = _____

2 x 80 = _____

3 x 80 = _____

8 x 80 = _____

5 x 40 = _____

❻ 6 x 40 = _____

40 x 8 = _____

5 x 40 = _____

7 x 40 = _____

2 x 160 = _____

 Tell about the patterns in Problem 5.

Name _____ Date _____

Complete the multiplication table.

x	0	1	2	3	4	5	6	7	8	9	10
0	0		0		0		0	0		0	0
10	0	10	20	30		50		70			
20	0	20	40		80						200
30	0	30		90				210		270	
40	0		80				280				
50	0	50								450	
60	0		120				360				
70	0	70		210				490			
80	0			240					640		
90	0						540				
100	0			300							1,000

☆ Write about how this table is different from the table on page 62.

STAAR Mathematics Practice Grade 3 • ©2013 Newmark Learning, LLC

Name _____ **Date** _____

Solve.

1 Lara has 4 fifty-dollar bills. How much money does Lara have?

2 Jamie scored 20 points in the basketball game. Tyler scored twice that amount. How many points did Tyler score?

3 Complete the pattern in the table below.

Number of Centimeters	25	30	35	40	45	50
Number of Millimeters	250	300	350			

Circle the letter for the correct answer.

4 Julie works 30 hours per week. How many hours does she work in 9 weeks?

    A 39 hours

    B 390 hours

    C 360 hours

    D 270 hours

5 There are 40 students riding on each bus. There are 5 buses. How many students are riding on the buses?

    A 45 students

    B 200 students

    C 20 students

    D 245 students

Unit 12 Mini-Lesson ★
Solve Multiplication Problems

Standard

> ## I. Number, Operations, and Quantitative Reasoning
>
> **Solve Multiplication Problems**
>
> **3.4B (RS)** Solve and record multiplication problems (up to two digits times one digit).
>
> **3.14C** Select or develop an appropriate problem-solving plan or strategy, including drawing a picture, looking for a pattern, systematic guessing and checking, acting it out, making a table, working a simpler problem, or working backward to solve a problem.

Model the Skill

Hand out counters and write the following problem on the board.

> ### There are 3 flowers in each vase. There are 5 vases.
> ### How many flowers are there?

◆ **Say:** *Today we are going to solve different types of word problems. Look at the problem. How many flowers are there in each vase?* (3) *How many vases are there?* (5) *There are 5 groups of 3 flowers. How can we find how many flowers there are in all?* Have students share different strategies for finding the total number of flowers. (15; possible responses: count the flowers; find the total of 5 groups of 3)

◆ Use counters to demonstrate how to use repeated addition or multiplication to solve the problem. **Say:** *You can use repeated addition or multiplication to find the total number of flowers. The sum and the product will be the same.*

◆ Assign students the appropriate practice page(s) to support their understanding of the skill.

Assess the Skill

Use the following problems to pre-/post-assess students' understanding of the skill.

Ask students to complete each fact family.

5 x 6 = 30   4 x 9 = 36

_____ X _____ = _____   _____ X _____ = _____

_____ ÷ _____ = _____   _____ ÷ _____ = _____

_____ ÷ _____ = _____   _____ ÷ _____ = _____

Name _____ **Date** _____

Solve each problem.

1 Lisa has 5 rows of flowers. There are 5 flowers in each row. How many flowers are there?

_____ flowers

2 Sam has 3 baskets of apples. Each basket has 15 apples. How many apples does Sam have in all?

_____ apples

3 The grocer puts 12 carrots in each bag. If he sells 8 bags, how many carrots will he sell?

_____ carrots

4 Jane is making 2 peach pies. She puts 8 peaches in each pie. How many peaches does she need?

_____ peaches

5 Piper is making sandwich platters. Each platter will get 16 slices of cheese. If she makes 4 platters, how many slices of cheese will she use?

_____ slices of cheese

6 Tim is digging holes to plant seeds. He digs 18 holes. If he puts 4 seeds in each hole, how many seeds will he plant?

_____ seeds

☆ **Tell how you got your answers.**

Name _____ Date _____

Draw an array to solve each problem.

1 There are 3 rows of chairs.
There are 5 chairs in each row.
How many chairs are there?

_____ chairs

2 There are 8 rows of flowers.
There are 6 flowers in each row.
How many flowers are there?

_____ flowers

3 There are 2 vases.
There are 6 roses in each vase.
How many roses are there?

_____ roses

4 There are 6 rows of cookies.
There are 7 cookies in each row.
How many cookies are there?

_____ cookies

5 There are 4 rows of plants in
the garden. There are 11 plants
in each row. How many plants
are there?

_____ plants

6 There are 4 benches in the park.
Each bench has 6 seats. How many
seats are there?

_____ seats

7 Mike has 5 rows of corn.
He has 9 cornstalks in each row.
How many cornstalks does he have?

_____ cornstalks

8 David has 4 pouches. He wants to
put 15 marbles in each pouch.
How many marbles does he use?

_____ marbles

 Tell how you know when an answer is reasonable.

STAAR Mathematics Practice Grade 3 • ©2013 Newmark Learning, LLC

Name _____ Date _____

Solve.

1 Elena has 8 pairs of shoes. How many shoes does she have in all?

2 Anita bakes 3 pans of muffins. She put 9 muffins in each pan. How many muffins did she bake?

3 Dan builds a wall with blocks. He puts 6 blocks in each row. He builds 9 rows. How many blocks does he use?

4 Marco picked 3 baskets of apples. He put 14 apples in each basket. How many apples did he pick?

Circle the letter for the correct answer.

5 Lil has 4 pens. She has 5 times as many crayons. How many crayons does she have?

A 5 crayons

B 9 crayons

C 16 crayons

D 20 crayons

6 Dominic keeps his rock collection in a case. The case has 6 rows with 12 rocks in each row. How many rocks are in the case?

A 90 rocks

B 72 rocks

C 89 rocks

D 17 rocks

Unit 13 Mini-Lesson ★
Meaning of Division

Standard

I. Number, Operations, and Quantitative Reasoning

Meaning of Division

3.4C (RS) Use models to solve division problems and use number sentences to record the solutions.

Model the Skill

Hand out counters and write the following number sentences on the board.

$$2 + 2 + 2 = 6 \qquad 3 \times 2 = 6$$

◆ Discuss how addition and multiplication are related. **Say:** *Today we will see how subtraction and division are also related.* Have students use counters to model 3 groups of 2 and model each number sentence. Then have students use counters to model repeated subtraction.

$$6 - 2 - 2 - 2 = 0 \qquad 6 \div 2 = 3$$

◆ **Ask:** *How may counters did you start with?* (6) *What number did you subtract each time?* (2) *How many times did you subtract 2? You subtracted 2 until you got an answer of 0. You subtracted 2 three times. You can say that there are 3 groups of 2 in 6.*

◆ Remind students that the answer to a division problem is called the quotient. Help students connect the repeated subtraction to the division sentence. **Ask:** *What is the quotient of 6 ÷ 2?* (3)

◆ Assign students the appropriate practice page(s) to support their understanding of the skill.

Assess the Skill

Use the following problems to pre-/post-assess students' understanding of the skill.

$12 - 4 - 4 - 4 =$ _____

$12 \div 4 =$ _____

$12 - 6 - 6 =$ _____

$12 \div 6 =$ _____

Name _____ **Date** _____

Write the missing numbers.

❶

6 in all

2 equal groups

_____ in each group

6 ÷ 2 = _____

❷

12 in all

3 equal groups

_____ in each group

12 ÷ 3 = _____

❸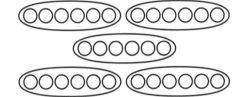

30 in all

_____ equal groups

_____ in each group

30 ÷ 5 = _____

❹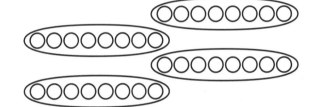

_____ in all

_____ equal groups

_____ in each group

_____ ÷ _____ = _____

❺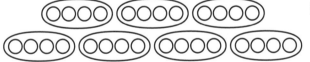

28 in all

_____ equal groups

_____ in each group

28 ÷ 7 = _____

❻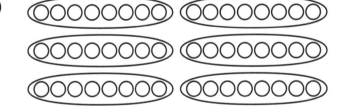

_____ in all

_____ equal groups

_____ in each group

_____ ÷ _____ = _____

 Tell what each number in the division sentence means.

Name _____ Date _____

**Use counters to model the problem. Draw rings to show the groups.
Write the missing numbers.**

1 4 in each group

_____ equal groups

8 ÷ 4 = _____

2 4 in each group

_____ equal groups

12 ÷ 3 = _____

3 2 in each group

_____ equal groups

12 ÷ 2 = _____

4 3 in each group

_____ equal groups

15 ÷ 3 = _____

5 3 equal groups

_____ in each group

6 ÷ 3 = _____

6 3 equal groups

_____ in each group

21 ÷ 3 = _____

7 2 equal groups

_____ in each group

10 ÷ 2 = _____

8 4 equal groups

_____ in each group

16 ÷ 4 = _____

 Tell how you solved each problem.

Name _____ **Date** _____

Solve.

1 We have 48 slices of pizza. Each whole pizza has 8 slices. How many whole pizzas do we have?

2 Jon has 3 equal rows of lemon trees. He has 27 lemon trees in all. How many trees does he have in each row?

3 The lake is 24 miles away. If we bike at 8 miles per hour, how long will it take to get to the lake?

4 There are 32 horseshoes in the barn. If each horse needs 4 horseshoes, how many horses can get new shoes?

Circle the letter for the correct answer.

5 Zach has 63 pages left in his book. If he reads 9 pages a day, how many days will it take him to finish his book?

A 9 days
B 8 days
C 7 days
D 6 days

6 The theater has 320 seats. There are 8 rows of seats. Which division sentence shows how many seats are in each row?

A 8 x 40 = 320 seats
B 320 x 8 = 40 seats
C 320 ÷ 40 = 8 seats
D 320 ÷ 8 = 40 seats

Unit 14 Mini-Lesson ★
Identify and Extend Patterns

Standard

II. Patterns, Relationships, and Algebraic Reasoning

Identify and Extend Patterns

3.6A (SS) Identify and extend whole-number and geometric patterns to make predictions and solve problems.

3.16A Make generalizations from patterns or sets of examples and non-examples.

Model the Skill

Draw the following figures on the board.

- ◆ **Say:** *We are going to look for patterns today. Look at these figures made from squares. How is the second figure different from the first?* (It has 3 more squares.) *How is the third figure different from the second?* (It has 3 more squares.) *How many squares should the next figure have?* (12)

- ◆ **Ask:** *How does the rule "add 3" help us understand the pattern?* (It describes how the pattern increases.) Have a volunteer extend the pattern by drawing the next two figures. (3 x 4 squares; 3 x 5 squares)

- ◆ Assign students the appropriate practice page(s) to support their understanding of the skill.

Assess the Skill

Use the following problems to pre-/post-assess students' understanding of the skill.

- ◆ **Ask:** *How would you complete the following patterns?*

  1, 3, 7, 15, 31, _____, _____, _____

  108, 90, 72, _____, _____, _____

Name _____ **Date** _____

Find the pattern. Complete the pattern for each problem.

 ❶

 ❷

 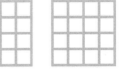

---

 ❸

7, 14, 28, 56, _____, _____

❹

625, 125, 25, _____, _____

---

 ❺

78, 65, 52, 39, _____, _____

❻

100, 52, 28, 16, _____, _____

---

❼

Input	Output
2	10
3	15
4	20

❽

Input	Output
2	8
3	12
4	16

---

❾

Input	Output
5	15
10	30
15	
	60

❿

Input	Output
2	7
4	13
6	19
8	

 Tell two ways to find the pattern in Problem 10.

Name _____ Date _____

Write the rule for each pattern. Then complete or extend the pattern.

1

Input	Output
2	12
5	15
7	17
13	

rule: _____

_____

2

Input	Output
3	12
6	24
9	36
12	

rule: _____

_____

3

Input	Output
4	12
6	18
8	24

rule: _____

_____

4

Input	Output
1	12
3	14
5	16
	18

rule: _____

_____

5

Input	Output
45	37
40	32
35	27

rule: _____

_____

6

Input	Output
48	4
36	3
24	2

rule: _____

_____

7

Input	Output
37	74
40	80
43	86

rule: _____

_____

8

Input	Output
68	34
58	29
48	24

rule: _____

_____

9

Input	Output
90	30
81	27
72	24

rule: _____

_____

10

Input	Output
13	31
14	33
15	35

rule: _____

_____

 Create your own pattern and define the rule.

STAAR Mathematics Practice Grade 3 • ©2013 Newmark Learning, LLC

Name _____ Date _____

Solve.

1 Use the following rule to make a pattern.

Rule: Add 9

_____

2 Use the following rule to make a pattern.

Rule: Multiply by 4

_____

3 Complete the pattern, then define the rule for the pattern.

1, 6, 11, 16, 21, _____, _____

Rule: _____

4 Complete the pattern, then define the rule for the pattern.

64, 53, 42, 31, _____,

_____

Rule: _____

Circle the letter for the correct answer.

5 Which of the following numbers complete the pattern below?

125, 100, 75, 50, _____, _____

    A 10, 5

    B 25, 5

    C 10, 2

    D 25, 0

6 Which of the following best describes the pattern below?

Input	Output
10	50
8	40
6	30
2	10

    A add 10

    B subtract 10

    C multiply by 5

    D divide by 5

Unit 15 Mini-Lesson ★
Patterns in Multiplication

Standard

> ## II. Patterns, Relationships, and Algebraic Reasoning
>
> **Patterns in Multiplication**
>
> **3.6B (SS)** Identify patterns in multiplication facts using pictorial models.

Model the Skill

Hand out counters and write the following problem on the board.

$$1 \times 3 = 3$$

◆ Have students use counters to model the problem. **Say:** *Today we are going to look for patterns when we multiply.* Have students model along as you demonstrate how to show 1 x 3 with counters.

◆ **Ask:** *How many groups of counters are there? How many counters are there in the group? What is the product of 1 x 3?*

◆ **Say:** *Now let's try multiplying other numbers by 1. What pattern do you see when we multiply with 1?* (Possible response: The product is always the other factor.)

◆ Follow a similar process for multiplying by zero. **Ask:** *Why don't you need counters to model 0 x 3?* (Possible response: because there are 0 groups of 3, which means you don't need any counters)

◆ Assign students the appropriate practice page(s) to support their understanding of the skill.

Assess the Skill

Use the following problems to pre-/post-assess students' understanding of the skill.

◆ Write the following patterns on the board and ask students to complete each pattern and then define the rule for each pattern.

2, 4, 6, _____, _____, 12, _____, 16 _____, 20

3, 6, _____, _____, 15, _____, 21 _____, 27, _____, 33, _____

16, 20, _____, 28, _____, _____, 40, 44

12, 18, _____, 30, _____, 42, _____, _____

STAAR Mathematics Practice Grade 3 • ©2013 Newmark Learning, LLC

Name _____ **Date** _____

Write each product.

**① **

1 x 0 = _____

1 x 1 = _____ □

1 x 2 = _____ ☆☆

1 x 3 = _____ ○○○

1 x 4 = _____ □□□□

1 x 5 = _____ ☆☆☆☆☆

1 x 6 = _____ ○○○○○○

1 x 7 = _____ □□□□□□□

1 x 8 = _____ ☆☆☆☆☆☆☆☆

**② **

0 x 1 = _____

0 x 2 = _____

0 x 3 = _____

0 x 4 = _____

0 x 5 = _____

0 x 6 = _____

0 x 7 = _____

0 x 8 = _____

0 x 9 = _____

**③ **

2 x 1 = _____ □□

2 x 2 = _____ ☆☆ ☆☆

2 x 3 = _____ ○○○ ○○○

2 x 4 = _____ □□□ □□□

2 x 5 = _____ ☆☆☆☆☆ ☆☆☆☆☆

2 x 6 = _____ ○○○○○○ ○○○○○○

2 x 7 = _____ □□□□□□□ □□□□□□□

2 x 8 = _____ ☆☆☆☆☆☆☆☆ ☆☆☆☆☆☆☆☆

**④ **

3 x 1 = _____

3 x 2 = _____

3 x 3 = _____

3 x 4 = _____

3 x 5 = _____

3 x 6 = _____

3 x 7 = _____

3 x 8 = _____

 Circle the pattern where the product is always zero.

Name _____ Date _____

Complete the multiplication table.

x	0	1	2	3	4	5	6	7	8	9	10
0	0		0		0		0	0		0	0
1		1	2	3		5		7			
2	0	2	4		8						20
3		3		9							
4	0		8					28			
5		5								45	
6	0						36				
7		7		21				49			
8	0								64		
9							54				
10	0			30							100

☆ **Write about the patterns you see in the table.**

STAAR Mathematics Practice Grade 3 • ©2013 Newmark Learning, LLC

Name _____ **Date** _____

Solve.

1 What is the product when one of the factors in a multiplication sentence is zero?

2 Which row in the multiplication table has the numbers 6, 12, 18, and 21?

3 Describe the pattern in the table below.

Number of Centimeters	1	2	3	4	5	6
Number of Millimeters	10	20	30			

Circle the letter for the correct answer.

4 There are 5 bookshelves. Each bookshelf has 8 books. Which expression can be used to show the total number of books?

A 8 + 5

B 8 + 8 + 8 + 8 + 8 + 8

C 8 x 5

D 5 x 5 x 5 x 5 x 5

5 There are 4 wheels on each stroller. The store has 20 strollers. How many wheels are in the stroller section of the store?

A 20 wheels

B 40 wheels

C 60 wheels

D 80 wheels

Unit 16 Mini-Lesson ★

Fact Families for Multiplication and Division

Standard	II. Patterns, Relationships, and Algebraic Reasoning

Fact Families for Multiplication and Division

3.6C (SS) Identify patterns in related multiplication and division sentences (fact families).

Model the Skill

Hand out counters and write the following problems on the board.

$$3 \times 4 = 12$$
$$12 \div 3 = 4$$

◆ **Say:** *Multiplication and division are opposite operations. That means they undo each other.* Demonstrate how to use counters to model 3 groups of 4. **Ask:** *How many groups of counters are there?* (3) *How many counters are in each group?* (4) *How many counters are there in all?* (12)

◆ Then demonstrate how to separate 12 counters into 3 equal groups. **Ask:** *How many counters did I start with?* (12) *How many groups did I make?* (3) *How many counters are there in each group?* (4) **Say:** *12 divided into 3 groups is 4 in each group.* Remind students that the answer to a division problem is called the quotient. Demonstrate how to record the quotient.

◆ Assign students the appropriate practice page(s) to support their understanding of the skill.

Assess the Skill

Use the following problems to pre-/post-assess students' understanding of the skill. Ask students to complete the following fact families.

$5 \times 6 = 30$

_____ x _____ = _____

_____ ÷ _____ = _____

_____ ÷ _____ = _____

$4 \times 9 = 36$

_____ x _____ = _____

_____ ÷ _____ = _____

_____ ÷ _____ = _____

Name _____ **Date** _____

Use counters. Complete each fact family.

❶

5 x 4 = 20

4 x 5 = _____

20 ÷ 5 = _____

20 ÷ 4 = _____

❷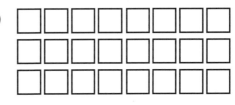

3 x 8 = 24

8 x 3 = _____

24 ÷ 8 = _____

24 ÷ 3 = _____

❸ 7 x 2 = 14

____ x ____ = ____

____ ÷ ____ = ____

____ ÷ ____ = ____

❹ 3 x 6 = 18

____ x ____ = ____

____ ÷ ____ = ____

____ ÷ ____ = ____

❺ 4 x 6 = 24

____ x ____ = ____

____ ÷ ____ = ____

____ ÷ ____ = ____

❻ 5 x 7 = 35

____ x ____ = ____

____ ÷ ____ = ____

____ ÷ ____ = ____

❼ 7 x 9 = 63

____ x ____ = ____

____ ÷ ____ = ____

____ ÷ ____ = ____

❽ 6 x 9 = 54

____ x ____ = ____

____ ÷ ____ = ____

____ ÷ ____ = ____

 Tell how you found the missing numbers.

Name _____ Date _____

Complete each fact family.

1 2 x 9 = 18

9 x 2 = _____

18 ÷ 2 = _____

18 ÷ 9 = _____

2 3 x 8 = 24

8 x 3 = _____

24 ÷ 3 = _____

24 ÷ 8 = _____

3 4 x 7 = 28

7 x 4 = _____

28 ÷ 7 = _____

28 ÷ 4 = _____

4 7 x 5 = 35

5 x 7 = _____

35 ÷ 7 = _____

35 ÷ 5 = _____

5 9 x 4 = 36

4 x 9 = _____

36 ÷ 9 = _____

36 ÷ 4 = _____

6 6 x 8 = 48

8 x 6 = _____

48 ÷ 8 = _____

48 ÷ 6 = _____

Use the numbers to write a fact family.

7 5, 6, 30

____ x ____ = ____

____ x ____ = ____

____ ÷ ____ = ____

____ ÷ ____ = ____

8 9, 3, 27

____ x ____ = ____

____ x ____ = ____

____ ÷ ____ = ____

____ ÷ ____ = ____

9 4, 6, 24

____ x ____ = ____

____ x ____ = ____

____ ÷ ____ = ____

____ ÷ ____ = ____

10 3, 7, 21

____ x ____ = ____

____ x ____ = ____

____ ÷ ____ = ____

____ ÷ ____ = ____

11 4, 8, 32

____ x ____ = ____

____ x ____ = ____

____ ÷ ____ = ____

____ ÷ ____ = ____

12 2, 8, 16

____ x ____ = ____

____ x ____ = ____

____ ÷ ____ = ____

____ ÷ ____ = ____

Name _____ **Date** _____

Solve.

❶ We have 42 oranges in 7 equal bags. How many oranges are in each bag?

❷ Each basket has 8 pears. We have 32 pears. How many baskets of pears do we have?

❸ Each bunch has 6 bananas. We have 42 bananas. How many bunches do we have?

❹ Marissa baked 4 apple pies. She used 8 apples in each pie. How many apples did she use?

Circle the letter for the correct answer.

❺ Which number sentence completes the fact family below?

$$7 \times 3 = 21$$
$$3 \times 7 = 21$$
$$21 \div 7 = 3$$

A $3 \times 7 = 21$

B $27 \div 7 = 9$

C $21 \div 3 = 7$

D $7 \div 3 = 21$

❻ Which of the following number sentences is not part of the fact family for 4, 6, and 24?

A $4 \times 6 = 24$

B $24 \div 6 = 4$

C $24 \div 4 = 6$

D $26 \div 4 = 4$

Unit 17 Mini-Lesson ★
Patterns in Tables and Charts

Standard

II. Patterns, Relationships, and Algebraic Reasoning

Patterns in Tables and Charts

3.7A (SS) Generate a table of paired numbers based on a real-life situation such as insects and legs.

3.7B (RS) Identify and describe patterns in a table of related number pairs based on a meaningful problem and extend the table.

Model the Skill

Show the following data table.

Number of Bicycles	Number of Tires
1	2
2	4
3	6
4	8
5	?

◆ **Say:** *You can use a table to show data. We can also look at tables and find patterns within the data. The table here shows the number of bicycles and the number of tires.* **Ask:** *According to the table, how many tires would be on 5 bicycles?* (10) *What is the rule for this pattern?* (add 2 tires for each 1 bicycle)

◆ **Say:** *The next table shows the number of cars loaded on a transport truck.* **Ask:** *According to the table, how many cars would fit on 4 transport trucks?* (36) *What is the rule for this pattern?* (add nine cars for each 1 truck)

Number of Trucks	Number of Cars
1	9
2	18
3	27
4	?
5	45

◆ Assign students the appropriate practice page(s) to support their understanding of the skill.

Assess the Skill

Use the following activity to pre-/post-assess students' understanding of the skill.

◆ Using items such as vehicles equipped with wheels (for example, bicycles, tricycles, cars, trucks), ask students to make a table and generate patterned data.

Name _____ **Date** _____

Complete each table.

Number of Bicycles	Number of Tires
1	2
2	
3	
4	
5	
6	
7	
8	
9	
10	

Number of Tricycles	Number of Tires
1	3
2	
3	
4	
5	
6	
7	
8	
9	
10	

Number of Cars	Number of Tires
1	4
2	
3	
4	
5	
6	
7	
8	
9	
10	

Number of Trucks	Number of Tires
1	6
2	
3	
4	
5	
6	
7	
8	
9	
10	

Name _____ Date _____

Look for patterns. Then complete each table.

1

Number of Bicycles	1	2	3	4	5	6
Number of Wheels	2	4	6			

2

Number of Nickels	1	2	3	4	5	6
Number of Cents	5	10	15			

3

Number of Chairs	1	2	3	4	5	6
Number of Legs	4	8				

4

Number of Insects	1	2	3	4	5	6
Number of Legs	6		18			

5

Number of Gallons	1	2	3	4	5	6
Number of Pints	8	16			40	

6

Number of Centimeters	1	2	3	4	5	6
Number of Millimeters	10	20	30			

7

Number of Tricycles	0	1	2	3	4	5
Number of Wheels	0	3				

8

Number of Skateboards	0	2	4	6	8	10
Number of Wheels	0	8				

 Tell about the patterns in Table 8.

Name _____ Date _____

Solve.

1 Sam has more than 50 cars in his toy car collection. He has started to make a table that shows the number of cars and the number of wheels. Complete the table.

Number of Cars	Number of Wheels
2	
4	
6	
8	
10	

2 Which rule best describes the pattern in Sam's table?

    A Add 2 wheels

    B Subtract 2 wheels

    C Add 8 wheels

    D Add 4 cars

3 How many wheels would 11 cars have?

    A 40

    B 36

    C 48

    D 44

Unit 18 Mini-Lesson ★

Describe and Compare Plane Figures

Standard

III. Geometry and Spatial Reasoning

Describe and Compare Plane Figures

3.8A (RS) Identify, classify, and describe two- and three-dimensional geometric figures by their attributes. The student compares two-dimensional figures, three-dimensional figures, or both by their attributes using formal geometry vocabulary.

Model the Skill

Draw the following.

♦ **Say:** *We are going to learn about quadrilaterals today. A quadrilateral is a plane figure with four sides. A plane figure is a closed figure—it begins and ends at the same place.* Have students identify the open and closed figures.

♦ **Ask:** *What shape is Figure 1?* (square) *How do you know the figure is a square?* (Possible response: It has four sides and four right angles.) *Is a square a quadrilateral? How do you know?* (Yes. It is a plane figure with four sides.)

♦ Have students look at the fifth figure. **Ask:** *What shape is this figure?* (open figure) *How many sides does this figure have? Is this figure a quadrilateral? Why or why not?* (No. It has 5 sides and it is not a closed figure.)

♦ Assign students the appropriate practice page(s) to support their understanding of the skill.

Assess the Skill

Use the following problems to pre-/post-assess students' understanding of the skill.

Have students draw a:

- square
- rhombus

- rectangle
- trapezoid

Name _____ **Date** _____

Draw a ring around each quadrilateral.

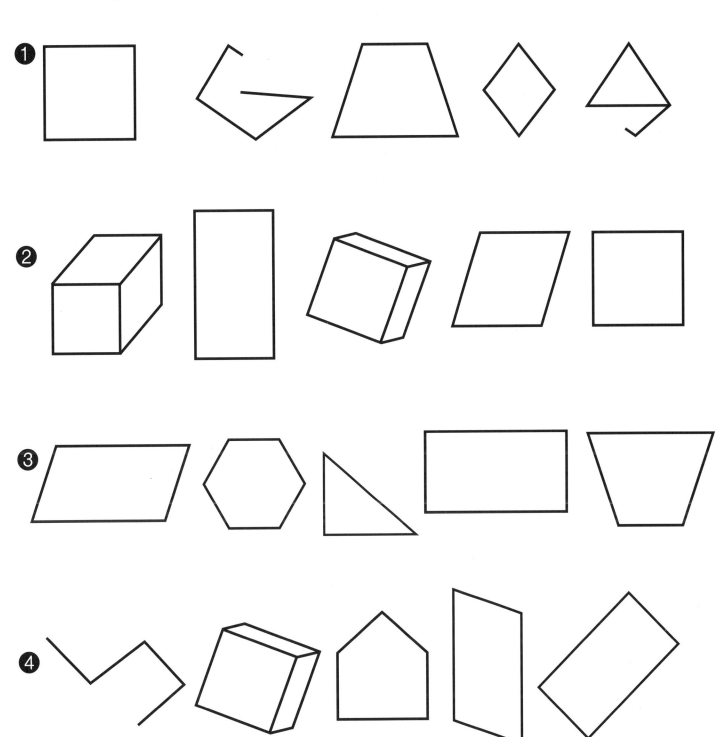

Name _____ Date _____

Cross out the figures that do NOT belong.

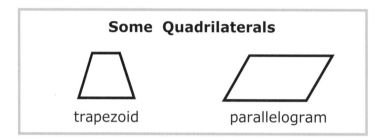

Some Quadrilaterals

trapezoid   parallelogram

1 trapezoids

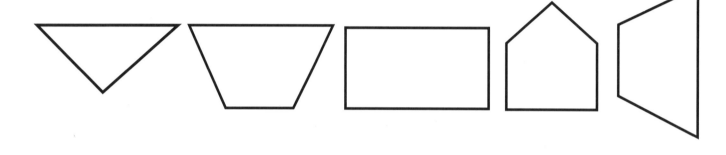

2 squares

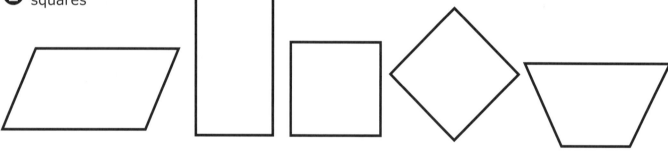

3 rectangles

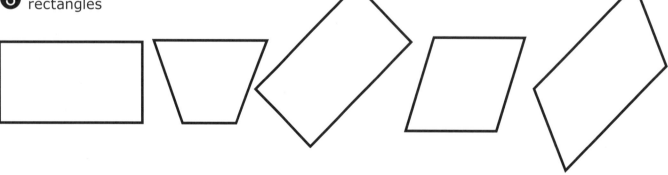

☆   **Tell how a rectangle and a trapezoid are different.**

Name _____ **Date** _____

Draw each figure.

❶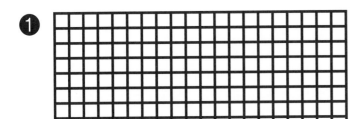

Draw a quadrilateral with
4 sides of equal lengths.

❷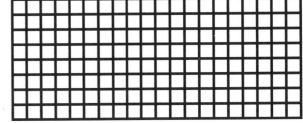

Draw a quadrilateral that is
NOT a rectangle.

❸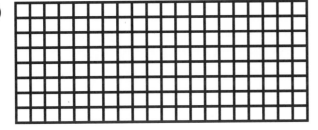

Draw a quadrilateral that does NOT
have 4 right angles.

❹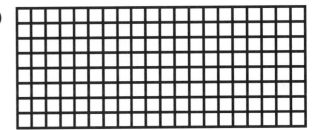

Draw a rhombus.

❺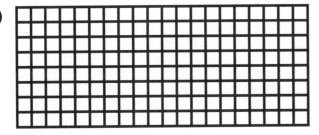

Draw a quadrilateral that is
NOT a square.

❻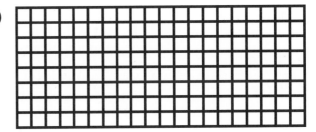

Draw a quadrilateral that has
2 sides of equal length and
no right angles.

Unit 19 Mini-Lesson ★

Describe and Compare Solid Figures

Standard

III. Geometry and Spatial Reasoning

Describe and Compare Solid Figures

3.8A (RS) Identify, classify, and describe two- and three-dimensional geometric figures by their attributes. The student compares two-dimensional figures, three-dimensional figures, or both by their attributes using formal geometry vocabulary.

3.14D Use tools such as real objects, manipulatives, and technology to solve problems.

Model the Skill

Hand out tangrams and solid figures.

◆ Display models of triangles, quadrilaterals, pentagons, hexagons, and cubes. **Ask:** *Which one of these shapes is most different from the other shapes?* (a cube) Hold up a cube and explain that it is a three-dimensional shape while the others are two-dimensional, or flat, shapes. **Ask:** *How many flat sides, or faces, does a cube have?* Have two volunteers work together to determine the number of faces. (6) **Ask:** *What shape are the faces of a cube?* (square)

◆ Hold up a triangle. **Say:** *Use a blue crayon to trace the sides of the triangle. How many sides did you trace?* (3) Allow tactile learners to touch the triangle models. **Say:** *To count the angles, use a red crayon to make a mark on each angle. How many angles are there?* (3) Explain to students that *tri-* means "three," and a triangle is a shape with three angles.

◆ Have students trace and mark the sides of a quadrilateral. **Say:** *Think about other words you know that begin with* quad. Quad *means "four." A quadrilateral has four sides and four angles.* Point out various quadrilaterals including a square, a rectangle, a rhombus, a trapezoid, and other parallelograms.

◆ Repeat with three-dimensional figures such as cubes, cones, spheres, rectangular prisms, triangular pyramids, etc.

◆ Assign students the appropriate practice page(s) to support their understanding of the skill. Guide students to link the names of each shape to the number of sides and angles of each shape.

Assess the Skill

Have students pick up handfuls of tangram shapes and ask them to trace and name each one.

Name _____ Date _____

List the number of faces for each figure. Then list the number of vertices.

❶ **square pyramid**

faces _____

vertices _____

❷ **rectangular prism**

faces _____

vertices _____

❸ **cylinder**

faces _____

vertices _____

❹ **sphere**

faces _____

vertices _____

❺ **cube**

faces _____

vertices _____

❻ **triangular prism**

faces _____

vertices _____

☆ **Tell how you found the number of vertices.**

Name _____ **Date** _____

Label each shape.

❶

_____

❷

_____

❸

_____

❹

_____

❺

_____

❻

_____

❼

_____

❽

_____

❾

_____

❿

_____

⓫

_____

⓬

_____

☆ **Tell which figure has an equal number of vertices and faces.**

Name _____ **Date** _____

Draw each shape described. Write its name.

❶ I have four equal sides and four equal angles. What am I?

❷ I have six sides and six angles. What am I?

❸ I have two parallel sides and two acute angles. What am I?

❹ I have six faces and eight vertices. What am I?

❺ I have four faces and four vertices. What am I?

❻ I have four faces and six vertices. What am I?

☆ **Tell how you know which shape is described.**

Unit 20 Mini-Lesson ★
Identify Congruent Figures

Standard

III. Geometry and Spatial Reasoning

Identify Congruent Figures

3.9A (SS) Identify congruent two-dimensional figures.

Model the Skill

Draw the following:

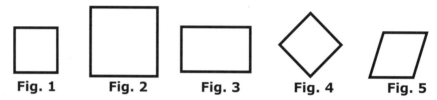

Fig. 1   **Fig. 2**   **Fig. 3**   **Fig. 4**   **Fig. 5**

◆ **Say:** *We are going to learn about similar and congruent figures today. Two figures that are similar are the same shape, but can be different sizes. Two figures that are congruent are the same shape and the same size.*

◆ **Ask:** *What shape is Figure 1?* (square) *How do you know the figure is a square?* (Possible response: It has four sides and four right angles.) *What figure is similar to Figure 1? How do you know?* (Figure 2, because it is also a square)

◆ **Ask:** *What figure is congruent to Figure 1?* (Figure 4) *How do you know?* (because it is the same shape and the same size.)

◆ Assign students the appropriate practice page(s) to support their understanding of the skill.

Assess the Skill

Use the following problems to pre-/post-assess students' understanding of the skill.

Have students identify the similar and congruent figures below.

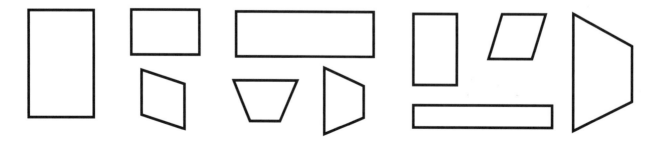

Name _____ Date _____

Circle the shapes in each row that are congruent.

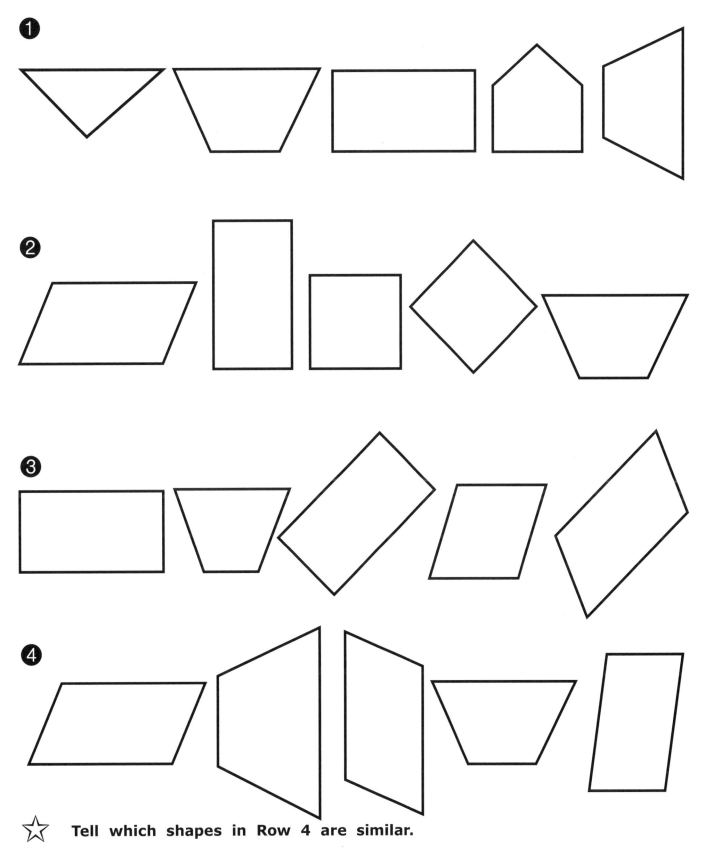

1

2

3

4

☆ **Tell which shapes in Row 4 are similar.**

Name _____ **Date** _____

Cross out the figures that are NOT congruent.

❶

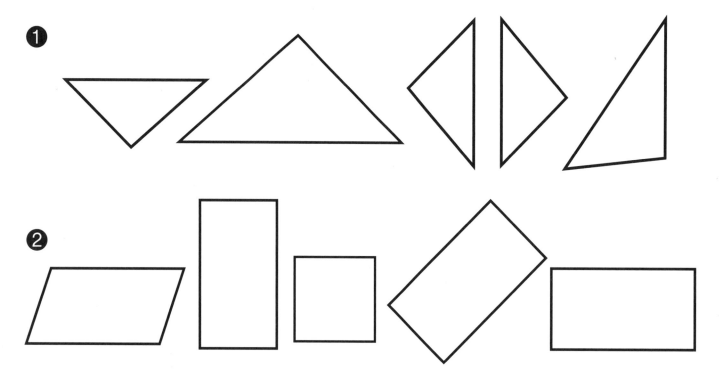

❷

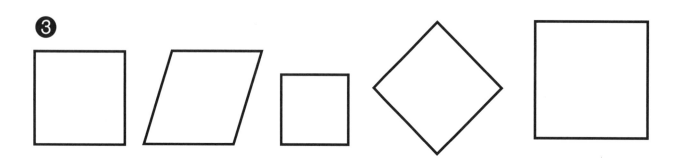

❸

❹

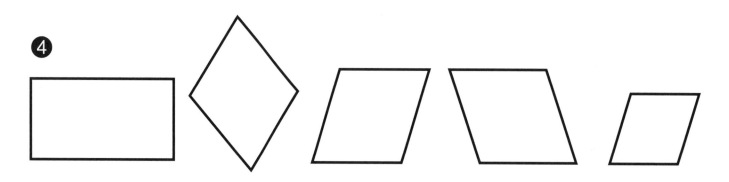

☆ **Explain the difference between congruent and similar.**

Name _____ **Date** _____

**Draw a ring around the congruent shapes in each row.
Then underline the similar shapes.**

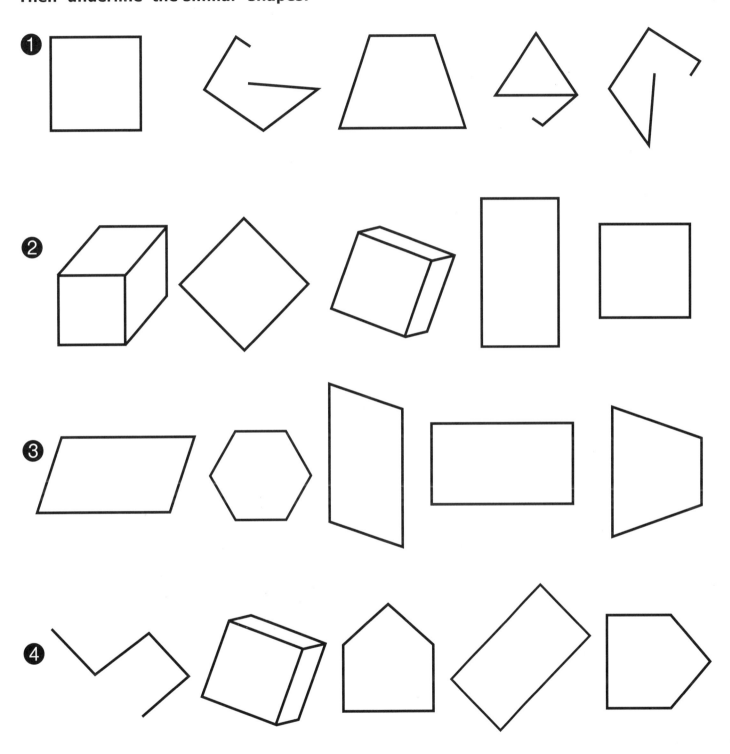

 Tell how you know which figures are not congruent.

Unit 21 Mini-Lesson ★
Identify Lines of Symmetry

Standard

III. Geometry and Spatial Reasoning

Identify Lines of Symmetry

3.9C (SS) Identify lines of symmetry in two-dimensional geometric figures.

Model the Skill

◆ **Say:** *We are going to cut shapes out of folded paper today to learn about symmetry. A line of symmetry divides a figure into two congruent parts.* Remind students that when two figures are congruent, they are exactly the same shape and same size.

◆ Help students draw a $\frac{1}{2}$ heart on a separate sheet of folded paper. Have students cut out the figure, being careful not to cut the fold. **Ask:** *What shape do you have when you unfold the paper?* (a heart) *The fold line is a line of symmetry. The fold divides the shape into two matching parts.*

◆ Help students complete the activity page, drawing the line of symmetry on the fold of each opened shape. Discuss why each shape is symmetrical. Discuss how both parts divided by the line of symmetry are congruent. If there is time, allow students to fold a paper twice and cut out a design.

Assess the Skill

Use the following problems to pre-/post-assess students' understanding of the skill.

◆ Ask students to draw as many lines of symmetry as they can for each figure.

Name _____ Date _____

Draw lines of symmetry for each figure. Write the total number possible for each figure.

1 ⬡ _____

2 E _____

3 _____

4 ⭐ _____

5 _____

6 ❀ _____

7 X _____

8 ▢ _____

☆ **Tell how you know where to draw the line of symmetry.**

Name _____ Date _____

Draw lines of symmetry for each figure. Write the total number possible for each figure.

①

_____

②

_____

③

_____

④

_____

⑤

_____

⑥

_____

⑦

_____

⑧

_____

⑨

_____

⑩

_____

⑪

_____

⑫

_____

☆ **Explain why Problem 5 has more lines of symmetry than Problem 10.**

Name _____ **Date** _____

Find the total number of lines of symmetry for each figure.

1

_____

2

_____

3

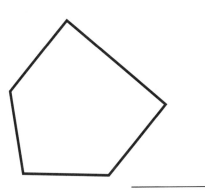

_____

4

_____

Circle the letter for the correct answer.

5 What is the total number of lines of symmetry for this shape?

A 2

B 4

C 6

D 8

6 What is the total number of lines of symmetry for this shape?

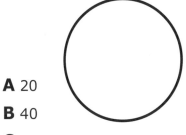

A 20

B 40

C 180

D 360

Unit 22 Mini-Lesson ★
Numbers on a Number Line

Standard

III. Geometry and Spatial Reasoning

Numbers on a Number Line

3.10A (RS) Locate and name points on a number line using whole numbers and fractions, including halves and fourths.

3.14C Select or develop an appropriate problem-solving plan or strategy, including drawing a picture, looking for a pattern, systematic guessing and checking, acting it out, making a table, working a simpler problem, or working backward to solve a problem.

Model the Skill

Draw the following number line.

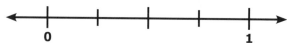

◆ **Say:** *You can use a number line to show fractions. Look at this number line. How does the number line show equal parts?* (Possible response: The tick marks are spaced equally.) *How many equal spaces are there?* Help students count each equal part of the number line to verify that there are 4 equal parts.

◆ Point out the 0 and 1 under the first and last tick marks. **Say:** *The number line shows one whole. Each space is one equal part of the number line. Since this number line is divided into 4 equal spaces, we can say that it shows fourths, or quarters.*

◆ Add tick marks to show eighths. **Ask:** *Now how many equal parts does this number line have? Which word tells how this number line is divided?* (eighths)

◆ Assign students the appropriate practice page(s) to support their understanding of the skill.

Assess the Skill

Use the following problems to pre-/post-assess students' understanding of the skill.

◆ Have students label the number line with the following points:
$\frac{1}{2}$, $\frac{1}{4}$, and $\frac{1}{8}$

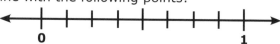

Name _____ Date _____

Draw a point on each number line to show the fraction.

1 $\dfrac{1}{2}$ 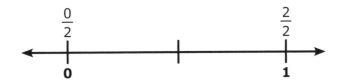

2 $\dfrac{1}{8}$ 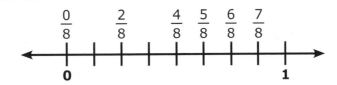

3 $\dfrac{1}{4}$ 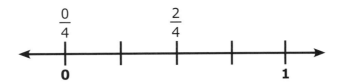

4 $\dfrac{1}{6}$ 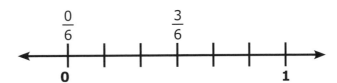

5 $\dfrac{1}{3}$ 

6 $\dfrac{3}{8}$ 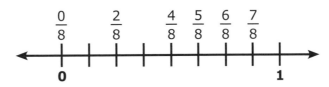

7 $\dfrac{3}{4}$ 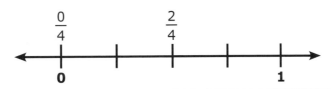

8 $\dfrac{5}{6}$ 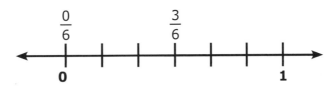

⭐ **Tell how you know the fraction matches the point on the number line.**

Name _____ **Date** _____

Write a fraction that names each point.

1
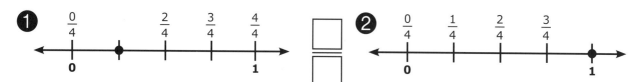

2
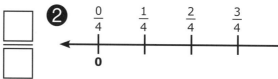

3

4

5
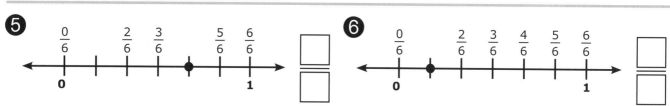

6

7
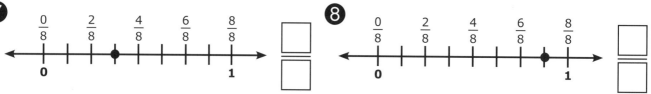

8
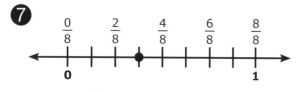

9
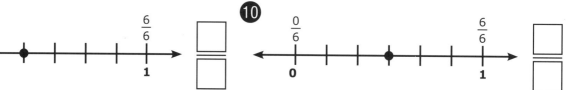

10
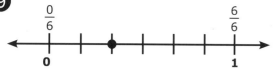

11
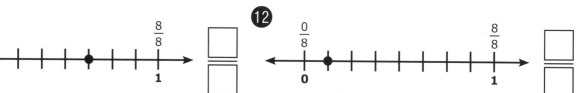

12

 Tell how you found the fraction to name the point on the number line.

STAAR Mathematics Practice Grade 3 • ©2013 Newmark Learning, LLC

Name _____ Date _____

Solve.

❶ Complete the number line.

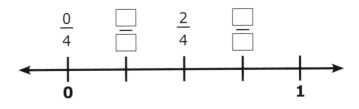

❷ Complete the number line.

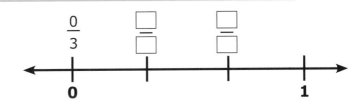

❸ Complete the number line.

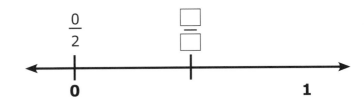

Circle the letter for the correct answer.

❹ Which number line shows $\dfrac{7}{8}$?

A

B

C

Unit 23 Mini-Lesson ★

Measure Length to the Nearest Quarter Inch

Standard

IV. Measurement

Measure Length to the Nearest Quarter Inch

3.11A (SS) Use linear measurement tools to estimate and measure lengths using standard units.

3.14D Use tools such as real objects, manipulatives, and technology to solve problems.

Model the Skill

Hand out rulers and unsharpened pencils.

◆ **Say:** *You can use an inch ruler to measure the length of an object.* Have students look at the ruler. Help them identify the $\frac{1}{4}$-inch and $\frac{1}{2}$-inch marks on the ruler. Point out that the $\frac{1}{2}$-inch mark is the same as $\frac{2}{4}$. Have students identify specific points on the ruler, such as $1\frac{1}{2}$ inches, $2\frac{1}{4}$ inches, and $4\frac{3}{4}$ inches.

◆ **Ask:** *What is the length of the unsharpened pencil to the nearest half inch?* ($7\frac{1}{2}$ *inches*) *How did you find your answer?* (Possible response: I looked for the number on the ruler that is closest to the end of the pencil.) *We can say the length of the ruler is $7\frac{1}{2}$ inches to the nearest half inch.*

◆ Assign students the appropriate practice page(s) to support their understanding of the skill.

Assess the Skill

Use the following problems to pre-/post-assess students' understanding of the skill.

◆ **Say:** *Estimate and then find the length of the following objects:*
- *a book*
- *a desk*
- *a tissue box*
- *a calculator*

Name _____ **Date** _____

Use an inch ruler. Measure each pencil to the nearest quarter inch.

1 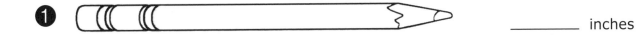 _____ inches

2 _____ inches

3 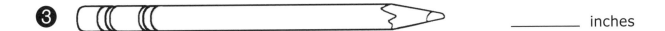 _____ inches

4 _____ inches

5  _____ inches

6  _____ inches

7  _____ inches

8 _____ inches

9 Use the data to make a line plot.

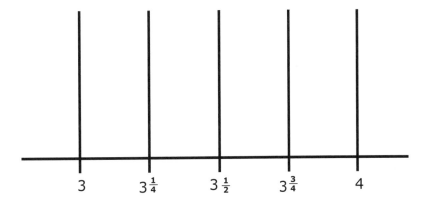

$3 \qquad 3\frac{1}{4} \qquad 3\frac{1}{2} \qquad 3\frac{3}{4} \qquad 4$

Length of Pencils in Inches

⭐ **Tell how you measured.**

Name _____ **Date** _____

Use an inch ruler. Measure the length of 10 crayons. Measure to the nearest quarter inch. Record the data. Use the data to make a line plot. Make an X to show the length of each crayon.

Crayon #	Crayon Length
1	
2	
3	
4	
5	
6	
7	
8	
9	
10	

Length of Crayons in Inches	Number of Crayons

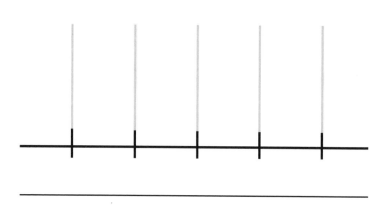

 Write an explanation of how the data in the chart matches the line plot.

Name _____ **Date** _____

Solve.

1 Sam measured the lengths of his crayons. The table shows his data. Use Sam's data to complete the line plot. Make an X to show each crayon and the length it measured.

Length of Crayons in Inches	Number of Crayons
3	|
$3\frac{1}{4}$	|||
$3\frac{1}{2}$	||||
$3\frac{3}{4}$	|
4	

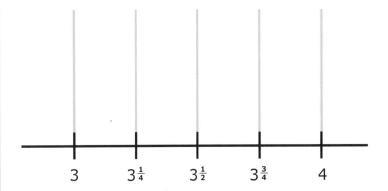

Length of Crayons in Inches

2 What length was the most common of Sam's crayons?

    A 4

    B $3\frac{3}{4}$

    C $3\frac{1}{2}$

    D $3\frac{1}{4}$

3 How many crayons were more than 3 inches in length?

    A 3

    B 4

    C 7

    D 9

Unit 24 Mini-Lesson ★
Find Perimeter

Standard

IV. Measurement

Find Perimeter

3.11B (RS) Use standard units to find the perimeter of a shape.

3.14B Solve problems that incorporate understanding the problem, making a plan, carrying out the plan, and evaluating the solution for reasonableness.

Model the Skill

Draw the following figures on the board.

Figure 1   Figure 2

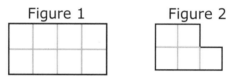

◆ **Say:** *Today we are going to learn about perimeter. Perimeter is the distance around a figure.* Have students look at Figure 1. Demonstrate how to find the length of each side.

◆ **Ask:** *What shape is this figure?* (rectangle) *What is the perimeter? How do you know?* (12 units; possible explanation: there are 12 units around the rectangle, so the perimeter is 12; add the length of each side)

◆ Have students look at Figure 2. **Ask:** *How is this figure different from Figure 1?* (Possible response: This is not a rectangle; this figure looks like a square with an extra square unit.) Point out that students can still tell the perimeter of the figure by counting the number of units on each side and adding. Help students find the length of each side.

◆ Assign students the appropriate practice page(s) to support their understanding of the skill.

Assess the Skill

Use the following problems to pre-/post-assess students' understanding of the skill.

◆ **Say:** *Find the perimeter of a book, your desk, a piece of paper. Draw a closed shape with a perimeter of 18 inches.*

Name _____ **Date** _____

Draw a closed figure. Write the perimeter.

❶

Perimeter: _____ units

❷

Perimeter: _____ units

Draw a closed figure to match the perimeter.

❸

Perimeter: 8 units

❹

Perimeter: 10 units

❺

Perimeter: 9 units

❻

Perimeter: 16 units

 Tell how you found the perimeter.

Name _____ Date _____

Add to find the perimeter.

❶

6 units

2 units   2 units

6 units

Perimeter: _____ units

❷

3 cm   3 cm

3 cm

3 + 3 + 3 = _____

Perimeter: _____ centimeters

---

❸

4 cm

3 cm   2 cm

5 cm

Perimeter: _____ centimeters

❹

4 ft

2 ft

4 ft

2 ft

6 ft

Perimeter: _____ feet

---

❺

3 cm   5 cm

4 cm

Perimeter: _____ centimeters

❻

4 ft

3 ft

5 ft

2 ft

6 ft

Perimeter: _____ feet

  Tell how you found the perimeter.

Name _____ **Date** _____

Solve.

1 A rectangle has a length of 8 units and a width of 3 units. What is the perimeter of the rectangle?

2 A square has a length of 16 units. What is the perimeter of the square?

3 The garden is a rectangle with a length of 20 feet and a width of 15 feet. What is the perimeter of the garden?

4 The rectangular floor has a length of 14 meters and a width of 11 meters. What is the perimeter of the room?

5 Ashley has a picture that is 11 inches tall and 8 inches wide. How much wood trim does she need to frame the perimeter of the picture?

A 27 inches

B 38 inches

C 40 inches

D 88 inches

6 The figure below is a diagram of John's yard. If John buys fence to run along the perimeter of his yard, how much fence will he need?

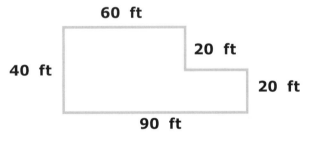

A 210 feet

B 230 feet

C 240 feet

D 260 feet

Unit 25 Mini-Lesson ★
Understand Area

Standard

IV. Measurement

Understand Area

3.11C (SS) Use pictorial models of square units to determine the area of two-dimensional surfaces.

Model the Skill

Draw the following figures on the board.

Figure 1   Figure 2

◆ **Say:** *Today we are going to learn about area. Area is the number of square units that are needed to cover a flat surface.* Have students look at Figure 1 and identify one square unit. **Ask:** *What figure do the square units make?* (rectangle) *You can count the square units in the rectangle to find its area. How many square units are in the rectangle?* (8) *We can say that the area of this rectangle is 8 square units.*

◆ Have students look at Figure 2. **Ask:** *How is this figure different from Figure 1?* (Possible response: This is not a rectangle; this figure has more sides, fewer square units.) Point out that students can still tell the area of the figure by counting the number of square units. (5) Allow students to use square tiles if they wish to model the figure and then find its area.

◆ Assign students the appropriate practice page(s) to support their understanding of the skill.

Assess the Skill

Use the following problems to pre-/post-assess students' understanding of the skill.

◆ **Say:** *Find the area of a tabletop, desktop, or a piece of paper. Draw a closed shape with an area of 18 inches.*

STAAR Mathematics Practice Grade 3 • ©2013 Newmark Learning, LLC

Name _____ **Date** _____

Draw a figure to match the area.

❶

4 square units

❷

9 square units

❸

8 square units

❹

12 square units

❺

14 square units

❻

18 square units

☆ **Tell how you know your figure shows an area of 12 square units.**

Name _____ **Date** _____

Add to find the area.

 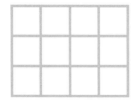

4 squares in each row, 3 rows

4 + 4 + 4 = _____

Area: _____ square units

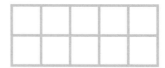

_____ squares in each row, _____ rows

5 + 5 = _____

Area: _____ square units

_____

Area: _____ square units

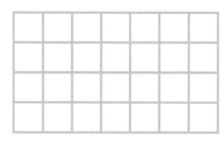

_____

Area: _____ square units

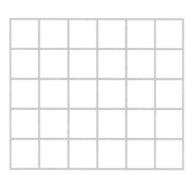

_____

Area: _____ square units

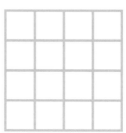

_____

Area: _____ square units

 Tell another addition sentence you can use to find the area.

Name _____ **Date** _____

Solve.

1 A rectangle has a length of 6 units and a width of 4 units. What is the area of the rectangle?

2 A square has a length of 5 units. What is the area of the square?

3 The rug is a rectangle with a length of 10 feet and a width of 8 feet. What is the area of the rug?

4 The tabletop has a length of 5 meters and a width of 2 meters. What is the area of the tabletop?

5 The gym floor has a length of 30 yards and a width of 20 yards. What is the area of the gym?

A 100 yards

B 100 square yards

C 600 yards

D 600 square yards

6 Esther's patio is 9 feet long and 7 feet wide. If Esther covers the patio in 1-square-foot tiles, how many tiles will she need?

A 16 tiles

B 32 tiles

C 63 tiles

D 126 tiles

Unit 26 Mini-Lesson ★
Measure Temperature

Standard

IV. Measurement

Measure Temperature

3.12A (SS) Use a thermometer to measure temperature (in degrees F).

3.14A Identify the mathematics in everyday situations.

Model the Skill

Show examples of a thermometer, including these drawn here.

◆ **Say:** *One way we measure temperature is by using a thermometer. These thermometers measure temperature on a scale of degrees Fahrenheit. A thermometer is a lot like a number line. We can use our understanding of number lines to read a thermometer. On this thermometer, each long tick mark is 10 degrees. Each short tick mark is 2 degrees.*

Thermometer A   **Thermometer B**

◆ **Ask:** *What temperature does Thermometer A read?* (80°F) *What temperature does Thermometer B read?* (22°F)

◆ Assign students the appropriate practice page(s) to support their understanding of the skill.

Assess the Skill

Use the following problems to pre-/post-assess students' understanding of the skill.

Ask students to identify the thermometers that show the warmest and coolest temperatures.

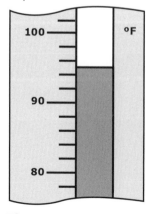

Thermometer A

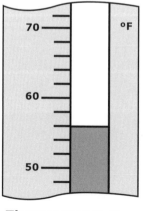

Thermometer B

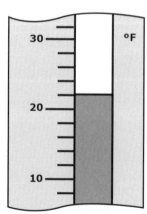

Thermometer C

STAAR Mathematics Practice Grade 3 • ©2013 Newmark Learning, LLC

Name _____ **Date** _____

Write the correct temperature for each thermometer.

1

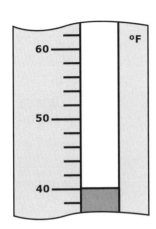

_____

2

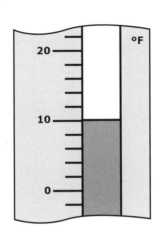

_____

3

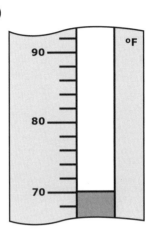

_____

4

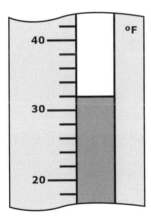

_____

5

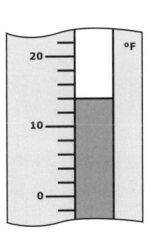

_____

6

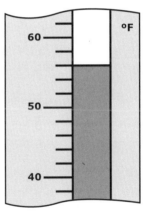

_____

☆ **Tell how you found the temperature.**

Name _____ **Date** _____

Write the correct temperature for each thermometer.

❶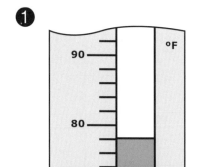

❷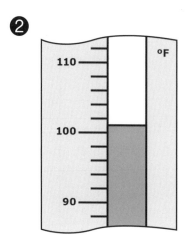

❸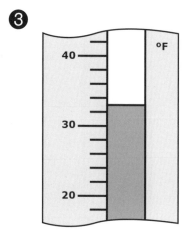

_____   _____   _____

Label each thermometer. Then shade it to show the correct temperature.

❹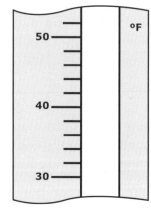

❺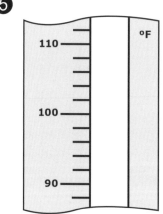

❻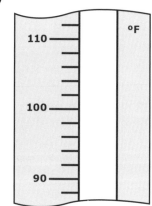

42 degrees   **98 degrees**   **103 degrees**

☆ **Tell how you found the number of degrees for each tick mark.**

Name _____ **Date** _____

1 What temperature is shown on the thermometer below?

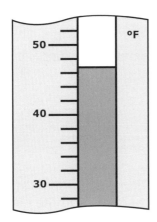

2 Label and shade the thermometer below to show a temperature less than 100 degrees.

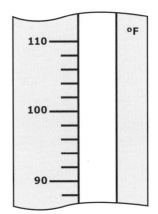

Circle the letter for the correct answer.

3 Which of the thermometers below shows a temperature greater than 110 degrees?

A   **B**   **C**   **D**

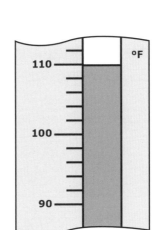

Unit 27 Mini-Lesson ★
Time to the Minute

Standard

IV. Measurement

Time to the Minute

3.12B (SS) Tell and write time shown on analog and digital clocks.

3.14A Identify the mathematics in everyday situations.

Model the Skill

◆ Display a demonstration analog clock. Review the parts of the clock. Have students identify the hour hand, the minute hand, and the numbers on the clock face.

◆ **Ask:** *How can we use a clock to tell time?* (Possible response: look at the numbers that the hour hand and the minute hand point to) **Say:** *The hour hand tells what hour it is. The minute hand tells how many minutes before or after the hour it is. There are 60 minutes in an hour. Each mark on the clock shows one minute. The marks on the clock can help us tell time to the minute.*

◆ Draw a clock that shows 10:15. **Ask:** *What number does the hour hand point to?* (10) *What number does the minute hand point to?* (15) *What time does the clock show?* (10:15) Demonstrate how to record the time. Remind students that the colon separates the hours from the minutes.

◆ Assign students the appropriate practice page(s) to support their understanding of the skill.

Assess the Skill

Use the following problems to pre-/post-assess students' understanding of the skill.

Ask students to tell the time shown on each clock to the minute.

Name _____ **Date** _____

Write the time two ways. Write the missing numbers.

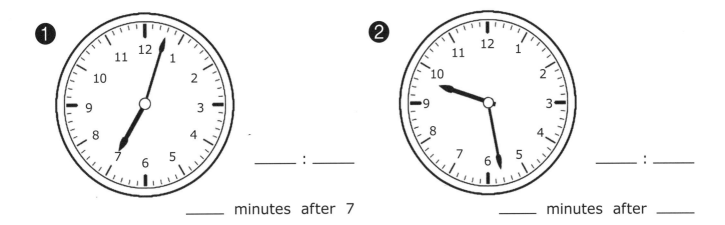

1 ____ : ____

____ minutes after 7

2 ____ : ____

____ minutes after ____

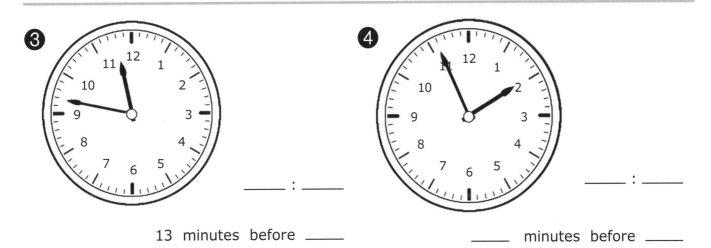

3 ____ : ____

13 minutes before ____

4 ____ : ____

____ minutes before ____

10 minutes later _____ : _____

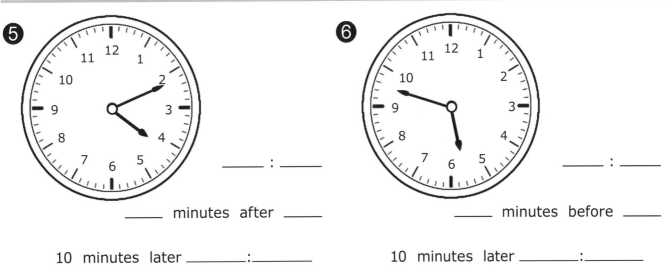

5 ____ : ____

____ minutes after ____

10 minutes later _____ : _____

6 ____ : ____

____ minutes before ____

10 minutes later _____ : _____

 Tell where the minute hand is pointing on Clocks 5 and 6.

Name _____ **Date** _____

Write the time. Then write the time 10 minutes later.

1  _____ : _____

_____ : _____

10 minutes later

2  _____ : _____

_____ : _____

10 minutes later

3  _____ : _____

_____ : _____

10 minutes later

4  _____ : _____

_____ : _____

10 minutes later

5  _____ : _____

_____ : _____

10 minutes later

6  _____ : _____

_____ : _____

10 minutes later

7  _____ : _____

_____ : _____

10 minutes later

8  _____ : _____

_____ : _____

10 minutes later

 Tell where the clock hands point when it is 10 minutes later.

Name _____ **Date** _____

Write how many minutes have passed.

Start at 4:00 A.M.
End at 4:22 A.M.
_____ minutes have passed.

Start at 8:30 A.M.
End at 8:45 A.M.
_____ minutes have passed.

Start at 10:40 P.M.
End at 10:56 P.M.
_____ minutes have passed.

Start at 2:58 A.M.
End at 3:07 A.M.
_____ minutes have passed.

Start at 8:10 A.M.
End at 8:42 A.M.
_____ minutes have passed.

Start at 11:50 A.M.
End at 12:02 P.M.
_____ minutes have passed.

Start at 9:31 P.M.
End at 9:49 P.M.
_____ minutes have passed.

Start at 1:07 A.M.
End at 2:00 A.M.
_____ minutes have passed.

Unit 28 Mini-Lesson ★
Make a Pictograph

Standard

V. Probability and Statistics

Make a Pictograph

3.13A (RS), 3.13B (SS) Collect, organize, record, and display data in pictographs and bar graphs where each picture or cell might represent more than one piece of data; interpret information from pictographs and bar graphs.

3.14B Solve problems that incorporate understanding the problem, making a plan, carrying out the plan, and evaluating the solution for reasonableness.

Model the Skill

Draw the following pictograph on the board.

Favorite Juices

Each ⊔ stands for 2 votes.

◆ **Say:** *Today we are going to learn about pictographs. Pictographs are graphs that use pictures or symbols to show information or data. What is the title of the graph?* (Favorite Juices) *What are the juice choices?* (apple, grape, and orange) *What does each cup stand for?* (2 votes) *How do you know?* (Possible response: The key under the graph tells you.)

◆ **Ask:** *Which juice got the most votes? How do you know?* (grape; possible explanation: it has the most cups/votes) Have students share their strategies.

◆ **Ask:** *How many students voted for orange juice?* (3) *How can you tell by looking at the graph?* (Possible response: I see there is a half cup, which would mean half of 2, which is 1.)

◆ **Ask:** *How many more students voted for grape juice than orange juice?* (1) Have students discuss other strategies such as subtracting the number of votes for orange juice from the number of votes for grape juice.

◆ Assign students the appropriate practice page(s) to support their understanding of the skill.

Assess the Skill

Use the following problem to pre-/post-assess students' understanding of the skill.

◆ **Say:** *Interview your classmates. Ask them to vote on their favorite sandwich or favorite fruit. Then share the data in a pictograph.*

Name _____ **Date** _____

Complete each pictograph. Then answer the questions.

1 Lea sold 14 tickets to the class play. Kim sold 8 tickets. Tom sold 12 tickets.

5 Addy sold 5 apples at the fair. Casey sold 10 apples. Finn sold 12 apples.

Tickets Sold

Lea	ADMIT ONE ADMIT ONE ADMIT ONE ADMIT ON
Kim	
Tom	

Each [ADMIT ONE] stands for 4 tickets.

Apples Sold

Addy	🍎
Casey	
Finn	

Each 🍎 stands for 2 apples.

Use the graph to answer each question.

2 How many more tickets did Lea sell than Tom?

_____ more ticket(s)

3 How many fewer tickets did Kim sell than Tom?

_____ fewer ticket(s)

4 How many fewer tickets did Kim sell than Lea?

_____ fewer ticket(s)

Use the graph to answer each question.

6 How many more apples did Finn sell than Casey?

_____ more apple(s)

7 How many fewer apples did Addy sell than Finn?

_____ fewer apple(s)

8 How many fewer apples did Addy sell than Casey?

_____ fewer apple(s)

 Tell how you completed each pictograph.

Name _____ Date _____

Complete each pictograph. Then answer the questions.

1 Gina took a poll of favorite lunches in her class. Grilled cheese got 6 votes. Veggie burritos got 3 votes. Hamburgers got 4 votes and pizza got 11 votes.

Favorite Lunches

Each ☺ stands for _____ votes.

Use the graph to answer each question.

2 How many more votes did pizza get than hamburgers?

_____

3 How many more votes did grilled cheese get than hamburgers?

_____

4 How many fewer votes did veggie burritos get than pizza?

_____

5 Chris took a poll of favorite sports in his class. Soccer got 9 votes. Baseball got 12 votes. Football got 6 votes and basketball got 8 votes.

Favorite Sports

Each ☺ stands for _____ votes.

Use the graph to answer each question.

6 How many more votes did baseball get than soccer?

_____

7 How many fewer votes did football get than baseball?

_____

8 How many fewer votes did football get than basketball?

_____

 Explain how you made your key.

Name _____ **Date** _____

Complete each pictograph. Then answer the questions.

1 Renee sold 30 tickets to the school raffle. Bobby sold 40 tickets. Lizzy sold 35 tickets.

Tickets Sold

ADMIT ONE = _____ ticket(s)

5 Max got 8 votes for class president. Riley got 10 votes. Alisa got 7 votes.

Votes for Class President

☺ = _____ vote(s)

Use the graph to answer each question.

2 How many more tickets did Lizzy sell than Renee?

_____ more ticket(s)

3 How many fewer tickets did Renee sell than Bobby?

_____ fewer ticket(s)

4 How many fewer tickets did Lizzy sell than Bobby?

_____ fewer ticket(s)

Use the graph to answer each question.

6 How many more votes did Max get than Alisa?

_____ more vote(s)

7 How many fewer votes did Alisa get than Riley?

_____ fewer vote(s)

8 How many fewer votes did Max get than Riley?

_____ fewer vote(s)

Unit 29 Mini-Lesson ★
Make a Bar Graph

Standard

V. Probability and Statistics

Make a Bar Graph

3.13A (RS), 3.13B (SS) Collect, organize, record, and display data in pictographs and bar graphs where each picture or cell might represent more than one piece of data; interpret information from pictographs and bar graphs.

3.14B Solve problems that incorporate understanding the problem, making a plan, carrying out the plan, and evaluating the solution for reasonableness.

Model the Skill

Copy the following bar graph onto the board.

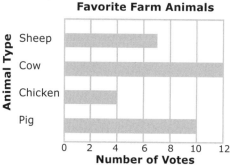

- ◆ **Say:** *Today we are going to learn about bar graphs. Bar graphs are graphs that use bars to show information or data. What is the title of this graph?* (Favorite Farm Animals) *What are the animal types?* (sheep, cow, chicken, pig) *What does each axis show?* (The x-axis, or horizontal axis, shows the number of votes and the y-axis, or the vertical axis, shows the type of animal.) *How do you know?* (Possible response: because each axis is labeled)

- ◆ **Ask:** *Which animal got the most votes? How do you know?* (cow; possible explanation: that bar is the longest) Have students share their strategies.

- ◆ **Ask:** *How many more students voted for pig than chicken?* (6) *How can you tell by looking at the graph?* Have students discuss other strategies such as subtracting the number of votes for chicken from the number of votes for pig.

- ◆ Assign students the appropriate practice page(s) to support their understanding of the skill.

Assess the Skill

Use the following activity to pre-/post-assess students' understanding of the skill.

- ◆ **Say:** *Interview your classmates. Ask them to vote on their favorite type of pet or favorite sandwich. Then share the data in a bar graph.*

Name _____ Date _____

Complete each bar graph. Then answer each question.

The students in the third grade voted for their favorite pet. Cat received 9 votes, dog got 14 votes, hamster got 6 votes, and fish got 10 votes.

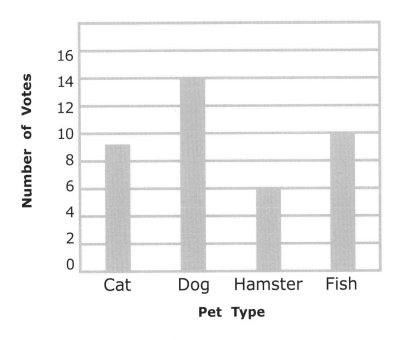

1 How many more students voted for cat than hamster?
_____ more student(s)

2 How many fewer students voted for fish than dog?
_____ fewer student(s)

3 How many more students voted for fish than cat?
_____ more student(s)

4 How many fewer students voted for hamster than dog?
_____ fewer student(s)

 Tell how you found your answers.

Name _____ **Date** _____

Complete each bar graph. Then answer each question.

1 Rachel sold 18 muffins at the bake sale. Perry sold 20 muffins. Kayam sold 25 muffins.

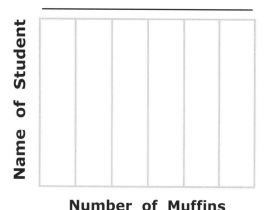

Number of Muffins

5 Buster read 40 pages over the weekend. Phoebe read 60 pages. William read 55 pages.

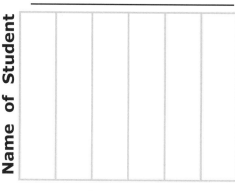

Number of Pages

Use your graph to answer each question.

2 How many more muffins did Perry sell than Rachel?

_____ more muffin(s)

3 How many fewer muffins did Perry sell than Kayam?

_____ fewer muffin(s)

4 How many fewer muffins did Rachel sell than Kayam?

_____ fewer muffin(s)

Use your graph to answer each question.

6 How many more pages did Phoebe read than William?

_____ more page(s)

7 How many fewer pages did Phoebe read than Buster and William combined?

_____ fewer page(s)

8 How many pages did they read in all?

_____ page(s)

 Write a description of how you completed the labels for each axis.

Name _____ **Date** _____

Complete each bar graph. Then answer each question.

1 Fred took a poll of favorite sandwiches in his class. Bologna got 10 votes. Tuna got 8 votes. Turkey got 7 votes and ham got 9 votes.

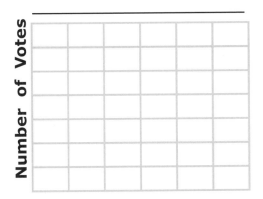

Type of Sandwich

5 The school store sold many items on Monday. The store sold 200 pairs of scissors, 400 notebooks, 500 pens, and 550 pencils.

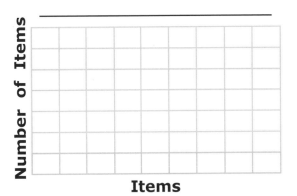

Items

Use your bar graph to answer each question.

2 What two sandwiches are the most popular?

_____ and _____

3 How many more votes did bologna get than turkey?

_____ more vote(s)

4 How many fewer votes did turkey get than ham?

_____ fewer vote(s)

Use your bar graph to answer each question.

6 How many more pencils were sold than pens?

_____ more pencil(s)

7 How many fewer scissors were sold than notebooks?

_____ fewer scissors

8 How many fewer scissors were sold than pencils?

_____ fewer scissors

Unit 30 Mini-Lesson ★

More Likely, Less Likely, Equally Likely

Standard	**Probability and Statistics** More Likely, Less Likely, Equally Likely **3.13C (SS)** Use data to describe events as more likely than, less likely than, or equally likely as.

Model the Skill

Draw a number line on the board as shown below. Display 3 white snap cubes and 1 red snap cube.

◆ **Say:** *The number line can show us how to describe an event, like picking a color without looking.*

◆ **Ask:** *If I pick one of these snap cubes without looking, which color am I more likely to pick?* (white) *Why?* (more white than red cubes) Draw a bar on the number line that covers $\frac{3}{4}$ of it and label it "white; more likely." *Which color am I less likely to pick?* (red) Label the $\frac{1}{4}$ of the line "red; less likely."

◆ **Ask:** *How likely is it that I will pick a blue snap cube?* (impossible) *What if all 4 of the snap cubes are white?* Show 4 white snap cubes. *How likely is it that I will pick a white snap cube?* (certain) Discuss other events that are impossible, certain, more likely, or less likely.

◆ **Say:** *Some events are equally likely.* Display 4 snap cubes: red, white, blue, green. **Ask:** *Why do you think it is equally likely to pick red as it is to pick white, blue, or green?* Guide students to see that each color is represented by the same amount, so no color has more cubes than any other. The amounts are equal. Draw a number line like the one above and label each fourth with a different color.

◆ Assign students the appropriate practice page(s) to support their understanding of the skill.

Assess the Skill

Use the following problems to pre-/post-assess students' understanding of the skill.

Have students use the spinner to determine whether each statement is true or false.

It is more likely that the spinner will land on circle than on triangle. (true)

It is less likely that the spinner will land on triangle than on circle. (true)

It is certain that the spinner will land on circle. (false)

It is impossible that the spinner will land on square. (true)

It is equally likely that the spinner will land on circle as on triangle. (false)

Name _____ **Date** _____

Complete. Write *more likely than*, *less likely than*, or *equally likely as*.

Event: Spin the spinner one time.

1 Landing on A is _____
landing on B.

2 Landing on D is _____
landing on C.

Event: Spin the spinner one time.

3 Landing on 3 is _____
landing on 6.

4 Landing on an odd number is _____
landing on an even number.

5 Landing on 6 is _____ landing on 2.

6 Landing on 2 is _____ landing on 3.

Event: Pick a coin from the bag without looking.
The bag has 2 pennies, 3 nickels, 2 quarters, and 1 dime.

7 Picking a penny is _____
picking a quarter.

8 Picking a dime is _____
picking a penny.

9 Picking a nickel is _____
picking a quarter.

 Tell how you would change the numbers on the spinner for Problem 3 to make landing on the number 6 certain.

Name _____ **Date** _____

Use the data in the table. Write *true or false* for each sentence.

Event: Pick a cube without looking.

1 Picking a red cube is less likely than picking a blue cube. _____

2 Picking a blue cube is equally likely as picking a green cube. _____

3 Picking an orange cube is impossible. _____

4 Picking a blue cube is certain. _____

5 Picking a red cube is equally likely as picking a green cube. _____

6 Picking a blue cube is more likely than picking a purple cube. _____

Snap Cubes in a Bag

Color	Number of Cubes
red	2
blue	5
green	2
purple	1

Use the spinner to answer each question.
Write *more likely than*, *less likely than*, or *equally likely as*.

7 Landing on B is _____ landing on D.

8 Landing on C is _____ landing on D.

9 Landing on C is _____ landing on B.

10 Landing on a triangle is _____ landing on a star.

11 Landing on a star is _____ landing on a circle.

12 Landing on a circle is _____ landing on a star.

 Tell how you know when two events are equally likely.

Name _____ Date _____

Solve. Use the spinner.

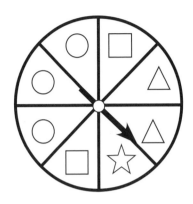

1 On which shape is the spinner less likely to land?
_____

2 On which two shapes is the spinner equally likely to land? _____ and _____

3 On which shape is the spinner most likely to land?
_____

4 The spinner is most likely to land on a shape that is not a circle. True or false?
_____

Circle the letter for the correct answer.

5 Two teams flip a coin to see which team gets the ball. The A Team chooses heads. The Q Team chooses tails. Which statement is true?

A Team A is more likely than Team Q to get the ball.

B Team Q is certain to get the ball.

C Team A is as likely to get the ball as Team Q.

D Team A is less likely than Team Q to get the ball.

6

Marbles in a Bag

Color	Number of Cubes
red	5
blue	3
green	8
purple	3

Sophie picks a marble from the bag without looking. Which statement is false?

A Sophie is most likely to pick a green marble.

B Sophie is least likely to pick a blue marble.

C Sophie is just as likely to pick a blue marble as she is to pick a purple marble.

D Sophie is less likely to pick red than green.

Grade 3 STAAR Mathematics Practice Assessment 1

Name _____ **Date** _____

Reference Materials

LENGTH

Customary

1 yard (yd) = 3 feet (ft)

1 foot (ft) = 12 inches (in.)

Metric

1 meter (m) = 100 centimeters (cm)

1 centimeter (cm) = 10 millimeters (mm)

TIME

1 year = 12 months

1 year = 52 weeks

1 week = 7 days

1 day = 24 hours

1 hour = 60 minutes

1 minute = 60 seconds

Centimeters

Inches

Solve.

1 What number rounds to 450 when it rounds to the nearest ten and 400 when it rounds to the nearest hundred?

A 451

B 454

C 405

D 446

2 Which problem has a sum of about 750?

A 507 + 296

B 984 − 228

C 429 + 322

D 356 − 312

3 The Puppy Palace used 138 flea collars in June. It used 142 flea collars in July. It used 206 in August. If the collars come in boxes of 100, how many boxes did the Puppy Palace need?

A 6

B 5

C 4

D 3

4 The lawn mower costs 456 dollars. The hedge clippers cost 179 dollars. How much more does the lawn mower cost?

 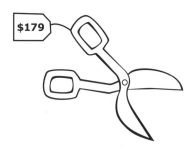

A 327 dollars

B 377 dollars

C 277 dollars

D 177 dollars

5 Majid has 4 rows of peach trees in his garden. Each row has 5 trees. If he plants one more row of 5 trees, how many peach trees will he have?

A 9

B 14

C 20

D 25

6 There are 8 trays of pies. Each tray has 9 pies. Which expression can be used to show the total number of pies?

A 8 + 9

B 9 + 9 + 9 + 9 + 9 + 9 + 9

C 9 x 8

D 8 x 8 x 8 x 8 x 8 x 8 x 8 x 8

---

7 There are 6 canoes on the canoe trip. There are 4 girls and 5 boys on each canoe. Which expression shows the total number of boys and girls on the canoe trip?

A 6 x (4 + 5)

B 4 x (6 + 5)

C (6 + 4) x 5

D 6 + 4 + 5

8 There are 8 wheels on each truck. The car and truck dealership has 10 trucks on display in the lot. How many truck wheels are on display in the lot?

A 18 wheels

B 20 wheels

C 40 wheels

D 80 wheels

9 The basketball team practices the same number of hours each week. The table below shows the total amount of time the players practice during different numbers of weeks.

Basketball Team Practice

Number of Weeks	Total Number of Hours
2	16
3	24
5	
8	64

How many hours do they practice in 5 weeks?

A 30 hours

B 32 hours

C 40 hours

D 44 hours

10 Catherine has 42 pages left in her book. If she reads 7 pages a day, how many days will it take her to finish her book?

A 8 days

B 7 days

C 6 days

D 5 days

---

11 Which number sentence completes the fact family below?

7 x 3 = 21
3 x 7 = 21
21 ÷ 7 = 3

A 3 x 7 = 21

B 27 ÷ 7 = 9

C 21 ÷ 3 = 7

D 7 ÷ 3 = 21

12 Dominic has 72 rocks in his collection. He keeps them in one full case with 8 rocks in each row. How many rows are in the case?

A 90 rocks

B 9 rows

C 7 rocks

D 7 rows

13 What number rounds to 870 when it rounds to the nearest ten and 900 when it rounds to the nearest hundred?

A 878

B 875

C 868

D 898

14 Which problem has a difference of about 500?

A 958 – 399

B 223 + 307

C 878 – 388

D 788 + 286

15 The seamstress needs 124 yards of fabric to complete the costumes for the first act of the play. She needs 378 yards of fabric to complete the costumes for acts two and three. How many yards of fabric does she need in all?

A 302

B 402

C 412

D 502

16 Gina's kitchen needs two repairs. The stove costs 450 dollars to repair. A new stove costs 679 dollars. The faucet costs 159 dollars to repair. A new faucet will cost only 89 dollars and 45 dollars to install. What is the least amount of money she can spend repairing or replacing the broken items in her kitchen?

A 377 dollars

B 609 dollars

C 768 dollars

D 584 dollars

17 Dari is planting a pumpkin patch in her garden. She plants 132 pumpkin seeds in all. If she plants 12 seeds in each row, how many rows of pumpkins will she have?

A 9

B 10

C 11

D 12

18 This graph shows the daily high temperature in Boulder, Colorado, for the first week in July. Which thermometer below shows the average high temperature for the first week in July?

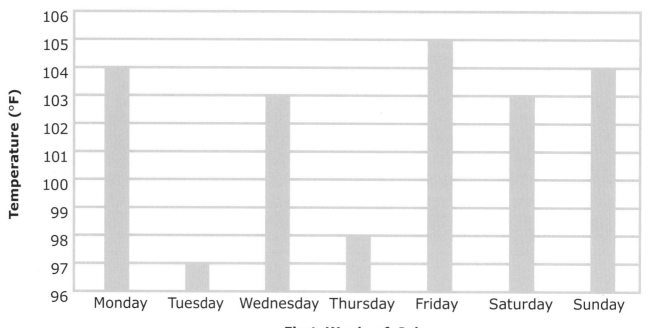

First Week of July

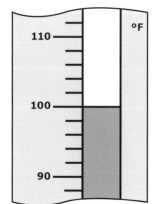
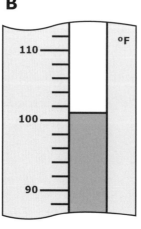
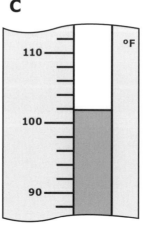
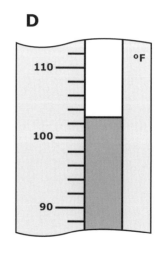

19 Clarissa swam 10 laps each weekday at camp. She was at camp for 6 weeks. Which expression shows the total number of laps she swam this summer?

A 6 x (10 + 5)

B 10 x (6 + 5)

C (7 x 6) x 10

D 10 x (6 x 5)

20 Ms. Baron's class did a poll on favorite snacks. The pictograph below shows the data results of the poll.

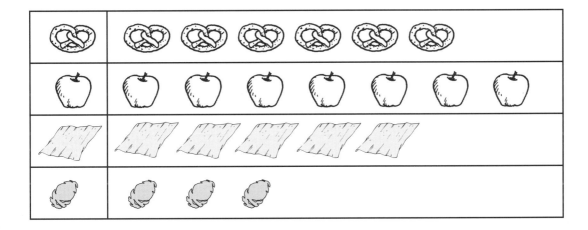

Which snacks were the least popular in Ms. Baron's class?

A crackers and raisins

B apples and raisins

C crackers and pretzels

D raisins and pretzels

21 Mr. Klein works 40 hours per week. If he has two weeks of vacation every year, how many hours does he work in a year?

A 3,000 hours

B 2,000 hours

C 300 hours

D 200 hours

22 Erin, Brett, Jake, and Ben biked a 100-mile relay race. They each biked an average of 20 miles per hour. It took about 3 minutes for each person to switch off their bikes. If each leg of the race is twenty-five miles, how long did it take them to complete the race?

A 2 hours, 12 minutes

B 4 hours, 9 minutes

C 5 hours, 12 minutes

D 5 hours, 9 minutes

STAAR Mathematics Practice Grade 3 • ©2013 Newmark Learning, LLC

23 Which digit would need to be written in the tens place in order to make this number greater than 375?

A 3
B 5
C 7
D 9

hundredths	tens	ones
3		4

24 Caden has $2.76 worth of coins in her piggy bank. Which combination of coins below could be in her piggy bank?

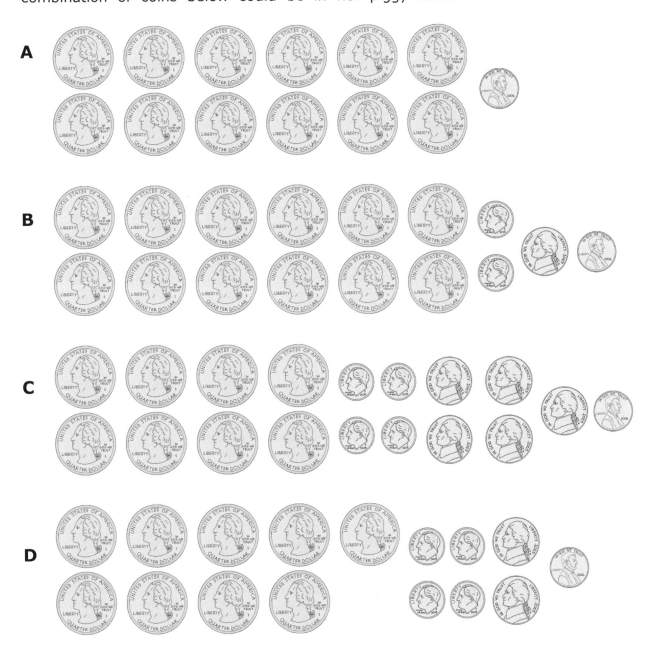

25 Which figure below shows $\frac{3}{4}$?

A

B

C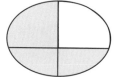

D

26 Which set below shows a value greater than $\frac{5}{8}$?

A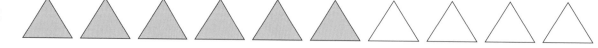

B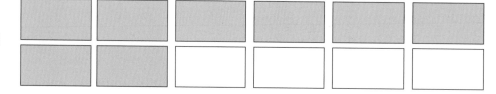

C

D

27 Pilar is framing a photograph that is 5 inches wide by 7 inches long. If she adds a 1-inch border around the entire photograph, how big a frame will she need?

A 4 x 6 inches

B 7 x 9 inches

C 6 x 8 inches

D 8 x 10 inches

28 Stan's laundry room is 8 feet wide and 12 feet long. If Stan wants to cover the entire floor with 1-square-foot tiles, how many tiles will he need in all?

A 84 tiles

B 96 tiles

C 40 tiles

D 48 tiles

29 Which figure best completes the pattern?

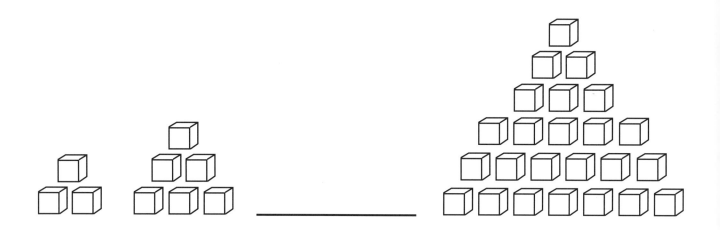

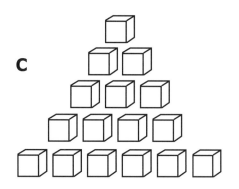

A

B

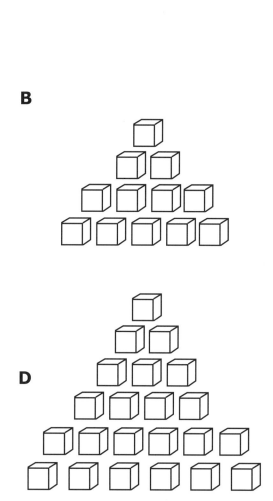

C

D

30 Karen has 50 ounces of juice in the pitcher. If each juice glass holds 6 ounces, how many full juice glasses can Karen pour?

A 6 glasses

B 8 glasses

C 9 glasses

D 5 glasses

31 Which combination of the shapes below would you need to make a square?

A

B

C

D

32 Angela has a chicken coop that has an area of 50 square feet. What is a possible perimeter of the coop?

A 30 feet

B 15 feet

C 25 feet

D 40 feet

33 Cecil weaves 4 baskets every 2 days. At this rate, how many baskets can he weave in 30 days?

A 15 baskets

B 30 baskets

C 60 baskets

D 120 baskets

140

STAAR Mathematics Practice Grade 3 • ©2013 Newmark Learning, LLC

34 Alex practices the violin the same number of hours each week. The table below shows the total amount of time he practices during different numbers of weeks.

Alex's Violin Practice

Number of Weeks	Total Number of Hours
2	28
3	42
6	
8	104

How many hours does he practice in 6 weeks?

A 56 hours

B 68 hours

C 72 hours

D 84 hours

35 The graph below shows the likelihood of rain in percentage during the coming 5-day forecast. If Sara and Liam want to go to the beach, what day would probably be the best day to go?

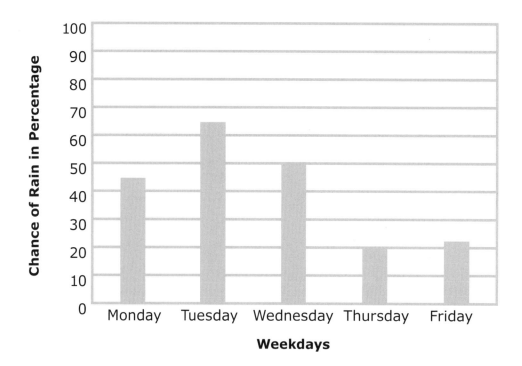

A Monday

B Tuesday

C Thursday

D Friday

36 Alicia made a friendship bracelet. Measure the length of the bracelet below and choose the answer that best describes its length.

A $6\frac{3}{4}$ inches

B $5\frac{1}{4}$ inches

C $6\frac{1}{2}$ inches

D $6\frac{1}{4}$ inches

---

37 Rodrigo's room has an area of 96 square feet. Which figure could represent the area of his room?

A

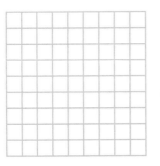

9 ft.

9 ft.

B

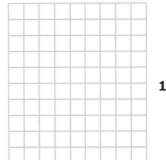

10 ft.

9 ft.

C

8 ft.

12 ft.

D

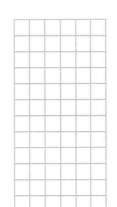

12 ft.

6 ft.

38 There are 500 marbles in the jar. 200 marbles are green. 130 marbles are blue and 170 marbles are red. If Jed is blindfolded and asked to draw a marble out of the jar, what is the probability that he will choose a green marble?

A 1 : 2

B 2 : 4

C 1 : 3

D 2 : 5

39 Tessa ate part of a cracker during snack time at school. The picture below shows how much of the cracker Tessa has left. How much of the cracker did she eat?

A $\frac{1}{4}$

B $\frac{4}{1}$

C $\frac{1}{3}$

D $\frac{3}{4}$

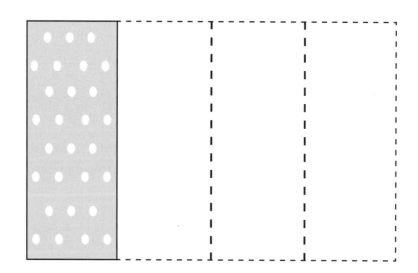

40 Which of the following numbers is NOT located correctly on the number line below?

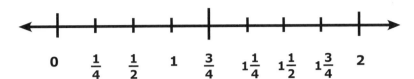

0    $\frac{1}{4}$ $\frac{1}{2}$ 1 $\frac{3}{4}$ $1\frac{1}{4}$ $1\frac{1}{2}$ $1\frac{3}{4}$ 2

A $\frac{1}{4}$

B 1

C $1\frac{1}{2}$

D 2

---

41 Look at the pattern of shaded triangles below.

Fig. 1

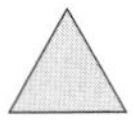

Fig. 2

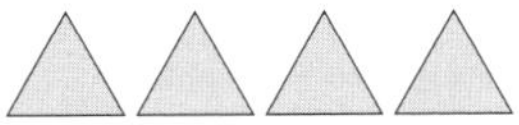

Fig. 3

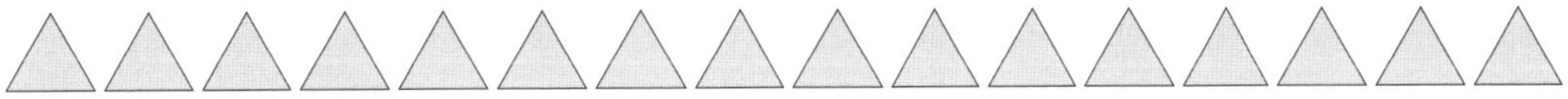

Fig. 4

If this pattern continues, what is the total number of shaded triangles that will be in Figure 4?

A 20

B 24

C 48

D 64

42 Vivian watched 45 minutes of television on Tuesday. She watched 22 minutes of her favorite show and 7 minutes of news. The rest of the time, Vivian watched commercials. How much time did Vivian spend watching commercials?

A 16 minutes

B 26 minutes

C 23 minutes

D 15 minutes

43 Alec has two figures on his desk. He writes a description of the figures that reads as follows:

- **Figure A has 4 vertices.**
- **Figure B has 4 faces.**

What two figures fit these descriptions?

A

C

B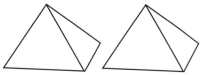

D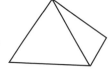

44 Fiona has three types of pets at home. She has 3 dogs. She has twice as many rabbits. She has 4 times as many fish as rabbits. How many fish does Fiona have in her home?

Record your answer and fill in the bubbles. Be sure to use the correct place value.

45 Gregor cut a 42-inch piece of ribbon to tie decorative bows. If the ribbon is 2 inches thick, what is the perimeter of the ribbon in inches?

Record your answer and fill in the bubbles.

Be sure to use the correct place value.

46 Henry, Stella, Baz, and McKenna are measuring their pencils. What is the combined length of their 4 pencils in centimeters?

Record your answer and fill in the bubbles. Be sure to use the correct place value.

Name _____ **Date** _____

Reference Materials

LENGTH

Customary

1 yard (yd) = 3 feet (ft)

1 foot (ft) = 12 inches (in.)

Metric

1 meter (m) = 100 centimeters (cm)

1 centimeter (cm) = 10 millimeters (mm)

TIME

1 year = 12 months

1 year = 52 weeks

1 week = 7 days

1 day = 24 hours

1 hour = 60 minutes

1 minute = 60 seconds

1 What number can round to 240 when it rounds to the nearest ten and 200 when it rounds to the nearest hundred?

    A 251

    B 254

    C 205

    D 243

2 Which problem has a sum of about 900?

    A 411 + 496

    B 1321 − 428

    C 536 + 288

    D 476 + 349

3 Jess had 574 stickers in her collection last year. She gave 65 to her cousin, Emma, last summer. Then she bought 125 more with her allowance over the school year. How many stickers does Jess have in her collection now?

    A 509

    B 619

    C 634

    D 734

4 Meg and Casey have the same amount of money. Meg has the bills and coins shown below. Which letter represents the amount Casey has?

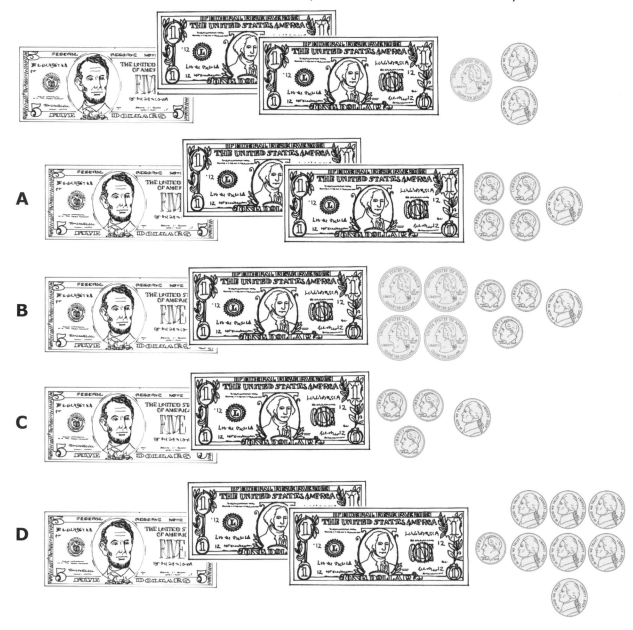

5 Kendall has four bookshelves. Each shelf has 12 books. If he takes 1 book off each shelf, how many books will be on the shelves?

A 11

B 44

C 47

D 48

6 The McCarthys had a pie for dessert on Sunday night. The picture below shows how much pie was left over. What fraction shows how much of the pie was eaten?

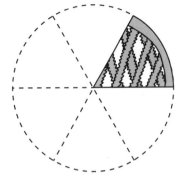

A $\frac{1}{6}$

B $\frac{2}{6}$

C $\frac{5}{6}$

D $\frac{6}{1}$

7 Jane had 1 hour to play between finishing her homework and setting the table for dinner. She played checkers with her older brother for 32 minutes. She played hopscotch for 15 minutes and she spent the rest of the time talking to her neighbor. Which equation shows how much time she spent talking with her neighbor?

A 60 − (32 + 15) = 13

B 60 − (32 − 15) = 13

C 60 − 32 − 13 = 15

D 32 + 15 + 13 = 1

8 There are 10 wheels on each moving truck. The moving truck rental company has 6 trucks in the lot. How many truck wheels are in the lot?

A 18 wheels

B 20 wheels

C 60 wheels

D 80 wheels

9 Rita and Tim have a chicken coop. The table below shows the total number of eggs one chicken produces during different numbers of weeks.

Egg Production

Number of Weeks	Total Number of Eggs
2	14
3	21
6	
8	56

How many eggs does the chicken lay in 6 weeks?

A 28 eggs

B 35 eggs

C 42 eggs

D 49 eggs

10 Melody has 8 math problems left on her math homework. If she solves 2 problems every 4 minutes, how many minutes will it take for her to finish her math homework?

A 8 minutes

B 10 minutes

C 12 minutes

D 16 minutes

11 Which number sentence completes the fact family below?

$9 \times 8 = 72$

$8 \times 9 = 72$

$72 \div 8 = 9$

A $72 \div 1 = 72$

B $72 \div 9 = 8$

C $72 \div 6 = 12$

D $72 \div 12 = 6$

12 There are 32 chess pieces in a game of chess. 2 are kings, 2 are queens, 4 are bishops, 4 are knights, and 4 are rooks. The rest are pawns. How many game pieces are pawns?

A 18

B 22

C 14

D 16

13 What number can round to 450 when it rounds to the nearest ten and 500 when it rounds to the nearest hundred?

A 456

B 445

C 461

D 452

14 Which problem has a difference of about 300?

A 758 – 399

B 123 + 211

C 574 – 288

D 688 + 386

15 The carpet installers have to cover the basement floor with 680 square feet of carpet. If the basement is a rectangle which formerly had a 9- by 12-foot rug, which of the following shows the most probable length and width of the basement?

A 20 feet x 34 feet

B 20 feet x 340 feet

C 2 feet x 340 feet

D 4 feet x 170 feet

16 Felice's printer is broken. A new printer will cost $128. To have her broken printer repaired will cost half the amount of a new printer. If she has the broken printer repaired, how much money will she save?

A $128

B $78

C $74

D $64

17 Orlando has 9 drawers in his dresser. If he puts 8 shirts in each drawer, how many shirts will he have in his dresser?

A 17

B 71

C 27

D 72

18 This graph shows the daily high temperature in Santa Fe, New Mexico, for the first week in May. Which thermometer below shows the average high temperature for the first week in May?

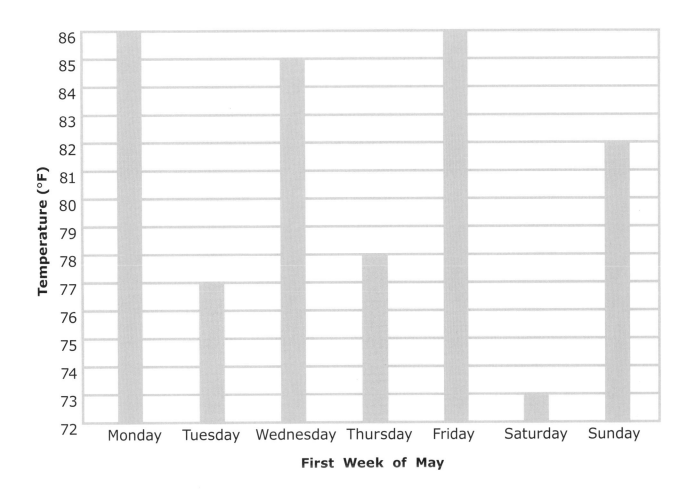

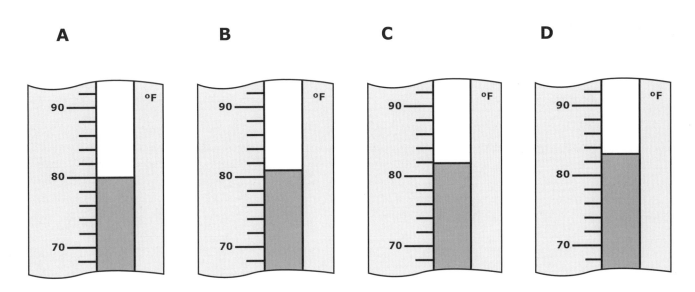

19 Jamie ran 5 miles on the track each weekday for soccer practice. He had practice for 8 weeks. Which expression shows the total number of miles he ran on the track?

A 5 x (5 x 8)

B 7 x (5 + 8)

C 7 + (5 x 8)

D 5 x (7 + 8)

20 Mr. Vasquez's class did a poll on favorite patterns. The pictograph below shows the data results of the poll.

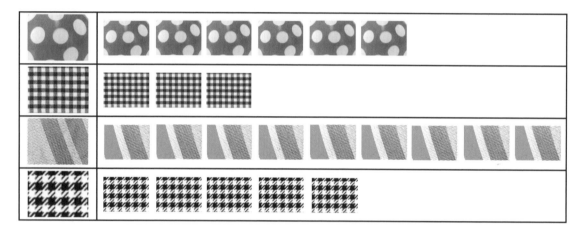

Which patterns were the most popular in Mr. Vasquez's class?

A polka dots and houndstooth

B stripes and houndstooth

C polka dots and stripes

D stripes and plaid

21 Ms. Adaro works 40 hours per week. If she has three weeks of vacation every year, how many hours does she work in a year?

A 120 hours

B 1,200 hours

C 1,960 hours

D 2,000 hours

22 Felix's family drove 135 miles on the parkway to visit their cousins during a vacation. If they averaged a speed of 45 miles per hour on the way there and back, how many hours did they drive on the parkway in total?

A 3 hours

B 4 hours

C 5 hours

D 6 hours

23 Which digit would need to be written in the tens place in order to make this number greater than 525?

hundreds	tens	ones
5		0

A 3

B 2

C 1

D 0

24 Camille has $3.90 worth of coins in her piggy bank. Which combination of coins below could be in her piggy bank?

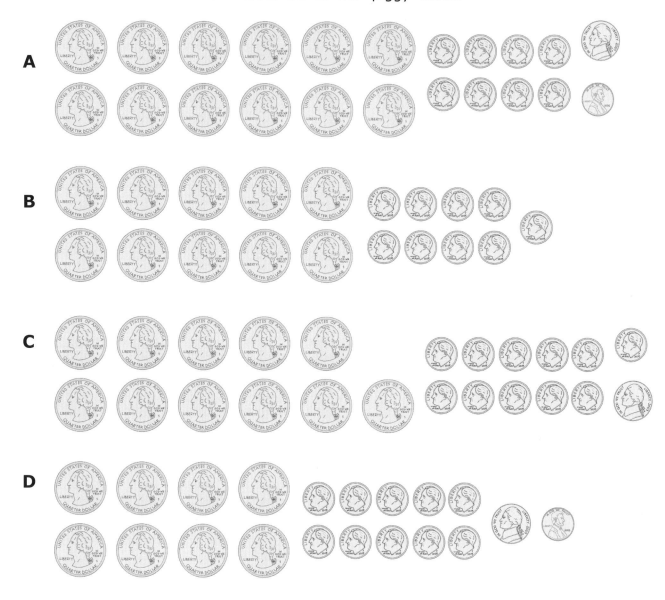

25 Which figure below shows $\frac{7}{8}$?

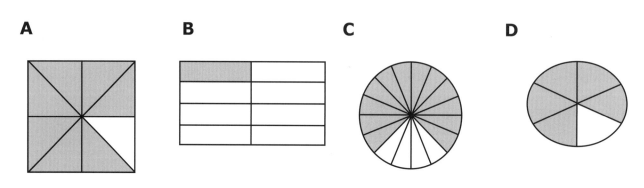

A   B   C   D

26 Which set below shows a value greater than $\frac{3}{4}$?

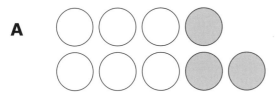

A

B

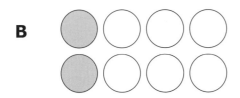

C

D

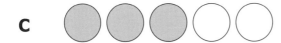

27 Danielle is building a fence to enclose the outer perimeter of her backyard. Use the diagram to find out how many feet of fence she will need.

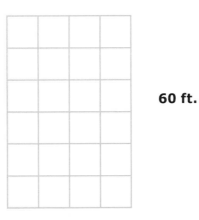

60 ft.

40 ft.

A 100 feet

B 120 feet

C 140 feet

D 200 feet

28 Rita's kitchen is 9 feet wide and 12 feet long. Rita wants to retile the entire floor and cover it with 1-square-foot tiles. If the tiles cost $10 each, how much will it cost to retile the floor?

A $96

B $108

C $960

D $1,080

29 Which figure best completes the pattern?

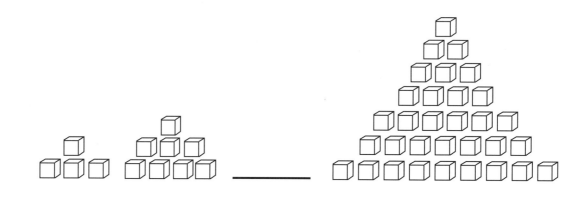

A

B

C

D

30 Audrey has a lemonade stand. She has 80 ounces of lemonade prepared. If each glass holds 8 ounces and costs 25¢, how much money can she earn selling lemonade?

A $2.00

B $2.50

C $5.00

D $10.00

31 Which combination of the shapes below would you need to make a triangle?

A

B

C

D

32 Fred has two vegetable gardens on his property. One is 6 feet by 11 feet. The other is 4 feet by 8 feet. What is the combined area of land that is covered with vegetable gardens on Fred's property?

A 106 square feet

B 108 square feet

C 96 square feet

D 98 square feet

33 Liza makes 40 pots per week. At this rate, how many pots can she make in 70 days?

A 20 pots

B 40 pots

C 400 pots

D 200 pots

34 William plays the guitar in his band the same number of hours each week. The table below shows the total amount of time he plays guitar during different numbers of weeks.

William's Guitar-Playing

Number of Weeks	Total Number of Hours
2	15
4	30
8	
10	75

How many hours does he practice in 8 weeks?

A 35 hours

B 45 hours

C 50 hours

D 60 hours

35 The graph below shows the likelihood of snow in percentage during the coming 5-day forecast. If Jaybez and Allie want to go skiing in fresh snow, what day would probably be the best day to go?

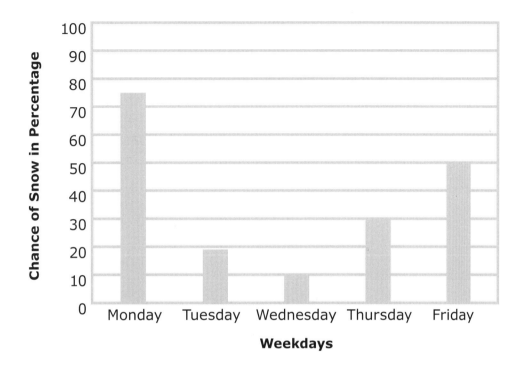

A Monday

B Tuesday

C Thursday

D Friday

36 Liam made a model train. Measure the length of the train below and choose the answer that best describes its length.

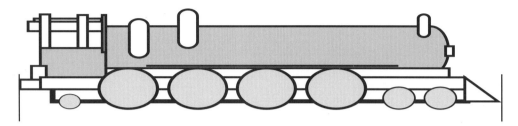

A $5\frac{3}{4}$ inches

B $5\frac{1}{4}$ inches

C $4\frac{1}{5}$ inches

D $6\frac{1}{4}$ inches

---

37 Natalie's quilt has an area of 80 square feet. Which figure could represent her quilt?

A

9 ft.

9 ft.

B
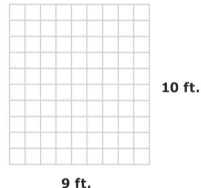
10 ft.

9 ft.

C

8 ft.

10 ft.

D
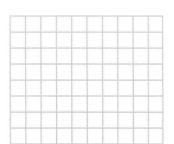
10 ft.

10 ft.

38 There are 600 pennies in the jar. If the probability of flipping a penny and getting heads is 1 in 2, and you flipped all 600 pennies, how many times would you probably get heads?

A 200 times

B 300 times

C 400 times

D 600 times

39 Owen ate part of a small pizza for lunch. His brother ate another part. The picture below shows how much of the pizza is left. How much of the pizza did they eat?

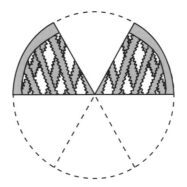

A $\frac{1}{4}$

B $\frac{2}{5}$

C $\frac{1}{3}$

D $\frac{6}{2}$

40 Which of the following numbers is NOT located correctly on the number line below?

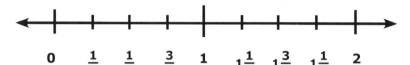

A $\frac{1}{4}$

B 1

C $1\frac{1}{2}$

D 2

---

41 Jillian painted the walls of her room blue and the ceiling white. What is the total surface area in square feet that she painted?

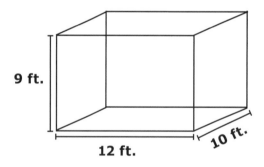

9 ft.

12 ft.

10 ft.

A 1,080 square feet

B 516 square feet

C 636 square feet

D 408 square feet

42 Bella read 72 pages of her book last week. She read 40 pages over the weekend, and then another 108 pages this week. If there are 304 pages in her book, how many more pages does she have left?

A 184 pages

B 84 pages

C 194 pages

D 94 pages

---

43 The sculpture in the park is a three-dimensional solid. It has 8 vertices and 6 faces.

What figure could NOT fit this description?

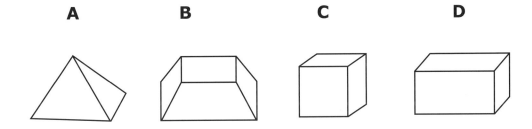

A   B   C   D

---

44 Cooper has 300 baseball cards. He puts 4 in each sleeve of his collection binders. He has 3 binders. How many protective sleeves does he have in all?

Record your answer and fill in the bubbles. Be sure to use the correct place value.

⓪	⓪
①	①
②	②
③	③
④	④
⑤	⑤
⑥	⑥
⑦	⑦
⑧	⑧
⑨	⑨

45 Look at the pattern of shaded circles below.

Fig. 1

Fig. 2

Fig. 3

Fig. 4

If this pattern continues, what is the total number of shaded circles that will be in Figure 4? Record your answer and fill in the bubbles. Be sure to use the correct place value.

46 Hilary, Sam, Katie, and Charlie are measuring lengths of string. What is the average length of their 4 strings in centimeters?

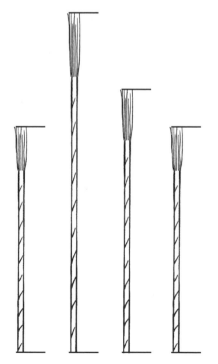

Record your answer and fill in the bubbles. Be sure to use the correct place value.

Answer Key (Units 1–4)

Unit 1 (p. 5)
1. 190; 100 + 90 + 0; one hundred ninety
2. 200 + 40 + 9; two hundred forty-nine
3. 628; six hundred twenty-eight
4. 834; 800 + 30 + 4
5. 600; 700; 800; 900
6. 490; 500; 510; 520
7. 525; 530; 535; 540
8. 660; 670; 680

Unit 1 (p. 6)
1. 700 + 30 + 2; seven hundred thirty-two
2. 594; five hundred ninety-four
3. 609; 600 + 0 + 9
4. 800 + 10 + 3; eight hundred thirteen
5. 340; 345; 350
6. 800; 900; 1,000
7. 770; 780; 790
8. 460; 465; 470
9. 750; 850; 950
10. 990; 995; 1,000

Unit 1 (p. 7)
1. 700 + 60 + 8; seven hundred sixty-eight
2. 470; 400 + 70 + 0
3. 660; 670; 680
4. 290; 300; 310
5. 960; 965; 970
6. 720; 725; 730
7. 450; 460; 470
8. 700; 705; 710
9. 840; 845; 850
10. 350; 360; 370
11. D   12. B

Unit 2 (p. 9)
1. 60   2. 620
3. 260 4. 400
5. 530 6. 400
7. 800 8. 300
9. 600 10. 1,000

Unit 2 (p. 10)
1. 310; 300
2. 770; 800
3. 450; 500
4. 920; 900
5. 690; 700
6. 70; 100
7. 630; 600
8. 110; 100
9. 550; 600
10. 245–249
11. 940
12. 465–474; 500

Unit 2 (p. 11)
Answers may vary.
1. range: 25–34
2. range: 50–149
3. range: 65–74
4. range: 350–449
5. B 6. D

Unit 3 (p. 13)
1. 21¢   2. 28¢
3. 26¢   4. 47¢
5. 46¢   6. 42¢
7. 100¢   8. 211¢

Unit 3 (p. 14)
1. $1.41   2. $0.65
3. $3.01   4. $2.06
5. $1.60   6. $0.41
7. $0.40   8. $1.26

Unit 3 (p. 15)
1. 32¢
2. 65¢
3. D
4. A

Unit 4 (p. 17)
1. 1/4 2. 1/3
3. 2/3 4. 1/2
5. 2/8 6. 1/8
7. 2/4 8. 1/2

Unit 4 (p. 18)
1. 3   2. 3
3. 5; 4/5 4. 2; 2/2
5. 1   6. 2
7. 5; 2/5 8. 2; 1/2

Unit 4 (p. 19)
1. 1/2
2. 1/3
3. 3/4
4. 3/8
5. D
6. D

Answer Key (Units 5–9)

Unit 5 (p. 21)

1. 500	2. 90	3. 460
4. 50	5. 870	6. 360
7. 570	8. 210	9. 960
10. 740	11. 80	12. 590
13. 250	14. 610	15. 850

Unit 5 (p. 22)

1. 470	2. 410	3. 620
4. 820	5. 170	6. 810
7. 720	8. 360	9. 320
10. 160	11. 940	12. 710
13. 740	14. 660	15. 460
16. 690	17. 670	18. 620
19. 540	20. 520	

Unit 5 (p. 23)

1. 140 beads

2. 310 baseball cards

3. 290 dollars

4. 220 stickers

5. B   6. C

Unit 6 (p. 25)

1. 468	2. 269	3. 367
4. 898	5. 123	6. 205
7. 304	8. 351	9. 801
10. 577	11. 569	12. 691
13. 621	14. 640	15. 723
16. 972		

Unit 6 (p. 26)

1. 599	2. 250	3. 461
4. 886	5. 377	6. 799
7. 790	8. 628	9. 975
10. 394	11. 716	12. 770
13. 762	14. 519	15. 879
16. 430	17. 527	18. 581
19. 709	20. 821	

Unit 6 (p. 27)

1. 507 dollars

2. 971 points

3. 798 craft sticks

4. 602 yards

5. A

6. B

Unit 7 (p. 29)

1. 215	2. 410	3. 136
4. 301	5. 121	6. 319
7. 120	8. 45	9. 363
10. 371	11. 390	12. 291
13. 664	14. 419	

Unit 7 (p. 30)

1. 124	2. 162	3. 375
4. 522	5. 189	6. 35
7. 336	8. 293	9. 52
10. 264	11. 109	12. 373
13. 231	14. 82	15. 49
16. 117	17. 196	18. 537
19. 335	20. 295	

Unit 7 (p. 31)

1. 151 dollars

2. 165 points

3. 77 craft sticks

4. 509 yards

5. B

6. D

Unit 8 (p. 33)

1. 9   2. 11

3. 7   4. 24

5. 16; 8; 24

Unit 8 (p. 34)

1. 7   2. 5

3. 15   4. 11

5. 18; 12; 24

6. 22; 112; 60

Unit 8 (p. 35)

1. 13 pieces of fruit

2. 9 green balloons

3. 5 miles 4. 12 muffins

5. A   6. D

Unit 9 (p. 37)

1. 12   2. 16

3. 15   4. 20

5. 12   6. 18

Unit 9 (p. 38)

1. 10   2. 20

3. 24   4. 16

5. 21   6. 36

Unit 9 (p. 39)

1. 15 apples

2. 12 plums

3. 18 miles

4. 24 muffins

5. C   6. D

Answer Key (Units 10–14)

Unit 10 (p. 41)
1. 8   2. 24
3. 16   4. 20
5. 35   6. 54
7. 32   8. 21

Unit 10 (p. 42)
1. 3 x 7 = 21;
   7 x 3 = 21
2. 4 x 8 = 32;
   8 x 4 = 32
3. (2 x 2) x 3 = 12;
   2 x (2 x 3) = 12
4. (2 x 4) x 3 = 24;
   2 x (4 x 3) = 24

5. (4 x 2) x 3 = 24;
   4 x (2 x 3) = 24
6. (2 x 3) x 3 = 18;
   2 x (3 x 3) = 18
7. 4; 45
8. 5; 18
9. Answers may vary.
10. Answers may vary.

Unit 10 (p. 43)
1. 8 x 7 = 56;
   7 x 8 = 56
2. 8 x 6 = 48;
   6 x 8 = 48
3. 5 x 4 = 20;
   4 x 5 = 20
4. 2 x 4 x 6 = 24;
   6 x 4 x 2 = 24, etc.
5. D   6. B

Unit 11 (p. 45)
1. 30; 60; 90; 120; 150
2. 180; 240; 210; 240; 240
3. 120; 180; 90; 180; 240
4. 160; 120; 80; 40; 0

5. 80; 160; 240; 640; 200
6. 240; 320; 200; 280; 320

Unit 11 (p. 46)
Check students' work.

Unit 11 (p. 47)
1. 200 dollars
2. 40 points
3. 400; 450; 500
4. D   5. B

Unit 12 (p. 49)
1. 25 flowers
2. 45 apples
3. 96 carrots
4. 16 peaches
5. 64 slices
6. 72 seeds

Unit 12 (p. 50)
1. 15   2. 48
3. 12   4. 42
5. 44   6. 24
7. 45   8. 60

Unit 12 (p. 51)
1. 16 shoes
2. 27 muffins
3. 54 blocks
4. 42 apples
5. D   6. B

Unit 13 (p. 53)
1. 3; 3   2. 4; 4
3. 5; 6; 6
4. 32; 4; 8; 32 ÷ 4 = 8
5. 7; 4; 4
6. 48; 6; 8; 48 ÷ 6 = 8

Unit 13 (p. 54)
1. 2; 2   2. 3; 4
3. 6; 6   4. 5; 5
5. 2; 2   6. 7; 7
7. 5; 5   8. 4; 4

Unit 13 (p. 55)
1. 6 pizzas
2. 9 trees
3. 3 hours
4. 8 horses
5. C   6. D

Unit 14 (p. 57)
1. Check students' work.
2. Check students' work.
3. 112; 224   4. 5; 1
5. 26; 13   6. 10; 7
7. 5; 25   8. 5; 20
9. 20; 45   10. 25

Unit 14 (p. 58)
1. 23; add 10
2. 48; multiply by 4
3. 10; 30; multiply by 3
4. 7; add 11
5. 30; 22; subtract 8
6. 12; 1; divide by 12

7. 46; multiply by 2
8. 38; divide by 2
9. 63; divide by 3
10. 37; multiply by 2
   and then add 5

Unit 14 (p. 59)
Answers may vary.
1. 9; 18; 27
2. 4; 16; 64
3. 26; 31; add 5
4. 20; 9; subtract 11
5. D   6. C

Answer Key (Units 15–17)

Unit 15 (p. 61)

1. 0; 1; 2; 3; 4; 5; 6; 7; 8

2. 0; 0; 0; 0; 0; 0; 0; 0

3. 2; 4; 6; 8; 10; 12; 14; 16

4. 3; 6; 9; 12; 15; 18; 21; 24

Unit 15 (p. 62)

Check students' work.

Unit 15 (p. 63)

1. 0

2. 3

3. multiply by 10

4. C

5. D

Unit 16 (p. 65)

1. 20; 4; 5

2. 24; 3; 8

3. 2 x 7 = 14; 14 ÷ 7 = 2; 14 ÷ 2 = 7

4. 6 x 3 = 18; 18 ÷ 6 = 3; 18 ÷ 3 = 6

5. 6 x 4 = 24; 24 ÷ 6 = 4; 24 ÷ 4 = 6

6. 7 x 5 = 35; 35 ÷ 7 = 5; 35 ÷ 5 = 7

7. 9 x 7 = 63; 63 ÷ 7 = 9; 63 ÷ 9 = 7

8. 9 x 6 = 54; 54 ÷ 9 = 6; 54 ÷ 6 = 9

Unit 16 (p. 66)

1. 18; 9; 2

2. 24; 8; 3

3. 28; 4; 7

4. 35; 5; 7

5. 36; 4; 9

6. 48; 6; 8

7. 6 x 5 = 30; 5 x 6 = 30; 30 ÷ 6 = 5; 30 ÷ 5 = 6

8. 9 x 3 = 27; 3 x 9 = 27; 27 ÷ 9 = 3; 27 ÷ 3 = 9

9. 4 x 6 = 24; 6 x 4 = 24; 24 ÷ 6 = 4; 24 ÷ 4 = 6

10. 3 x 7 = 21; 7 x 3 = 21; 21 ÷ 7 = 3; 21 ÷ 3 = 7

11. 4 x 8 = 32; 8 x 4 = 32; 32 ÷ 4 = 8; 32 ÷ 8 = 4

12. 2 x 8 = 16; 8 x 2 = 16; 16 ÷ 8 = 2; 16 ÷ 2 = 8

Unit 16 (p. 67)

1. 6 oranges

2. 4 baskets

3. 7 bunches

4. 32 apples

5. C

6. D

Unit 17 (p. 69)

1. 4; 6; 8; 10; 12; 14; 16; 18; 20

2. 6; 9; 12; 15; 18; 21; 24; 27; 30

3. 8; 12; 16; 20; 24; 28; 32; 36; 40

4. 12; 18; 24; 30; 36; 42; 48; 54; 60

Unit 17 (p. 70)

1. add 2

2. multiply by 5

3. multiply by 4

4. multiply by 6

5. multiply by 8

6. multiply by 10

7. multiply by 3

8. multiply by 4

Unit 17 (p. 71)

1. 8; 16; 24; 32; 40

2. C

3. D

Answer Key (Units 18–23)

Unit 18 (p. 73)
Check students' work.

Unit 18 (p. 74)
Check students' work.

Unit 18 (p. 75)
Check students' work.

Unit 19 (p. 77)
1. 5 faces; 5 vertices
2. 6 faces; 8 vertices
3. 3 faces; 0 vertices
4. 1 face; 0 vertices
5. 6 faces; 8 vertices
6. 5 faces; 6 vertices

Unit 19 (p. 78)
1. cube
2. triangular prism
3. triangular pyramid
4. sphere
5. rectangular prism
6. cube
7. parallelogram prism
8. square pyramid

9. cylinder
10. rectangular prism
11. cube
12. cone

Unit 19 (p. 79)
Check students' work.
1. square
2. hexagon
3. parallelogram
4. cube or rectangular prism
5. triangular pyramid
6. triangular prism

Unit 20 (p. 81)
Check students' work.

Unit 20 (p. 82)
Check students' work.

Unit 20 (p. 83)
Check students' work.

Unit 21 (p. 85)
Check students' work.

1. 6	2. 1
3. 1	4. 5
5. 1	6. 2
7. 2	8. 4

Unit 21 (p. 86)
Check students' work.

1. 2	2. 1
3. 0	4. 2
5. 3	6. 2
7. 4	8. 0
9. 1	10. 1
11. 4	12. 2

Unit 21 (p. 87)
Check students' work.
1. 2
2. 1
3. 1
4. 2
5. B
6. C

Unit 22 (p. 89)
Check students' work.

Unit 22 (p. 90)

1. 1/4	2. 4/4
3. 1/3	4. 2/3
5. 4/6	6. 1/6
7. 3/8	8. 7/8
9. 2/6	10. 3/6
11. 5/8	12. 1/8

Unit 22 (p. 91)
1. 1/4; 3/4
2. 1/2
3. 1/3; 2/3
4. A

Unit 23 (p. 93)

1. 3 3/4	2. 3
3. 3 1/2	4. 3 1/2
5. 3 1/4	6. 2 3/4
7. 3 1/4	8. 3 1/2

9. Check students' work.

Unit 23 (p. 94)
Check students' work.

Unit 23 (p. 95)
1. Check students' work.
2. C
3. D

Answer Key (Units 24–28)

Unit 24 (p. 97)
Check students' work.

Unit 24 (p. 98)
1. 16   2. 9
3. 14   4. 20
5. 12   6. 22

Unit 24 (p. 99)
Word Problems
1. 22 units
2. 64 units
3. 70 feet
4. 50 meters
5. B   6. D

Unit 25 (p. 101)
Check students' work.

Unit 25 (p. 102)
1. 12; 12
2. 5; 2; 10; 10
3. 15   4. 28
5. 30   6. 16

Unit 25 (p. 103)
1. 24 square units
2. 25 square units
3. 80 square feet
4. 10 square meters
5. D   6. C

Unit 26 (p. 105)
1. 40°F   2. 10°F
3. 70°F   4. 32°F
5. 14°F   6. 56°F

Unit 26 (p. 106)
1. 78°F   2. 101°F
3. 33°F
4. Check students' work.
5. Check students' work.
6. Check students' work.

Unit 26 (p. 107)
1. 47°F
2. Check students' work.
3. D

Unit 27 (p. 109)
1. 7:03; 3
2. 9:28; 28; 9
3. 11:47; 12
4. 1:56; 4; 2; 2:06
5. 4:11; 11; 4; 4:21
6. 5:48; 12; 6; 5:58

Unit 27 (p. 110)
1. 2:05; 2:15
2. 9:42; 9:52
3. 1:11; 1:21
4. 3:52; 4:02
5. 6:35; 6:45
6. 10:02; 10:12
7. 4:57; 5:07
8. 8:23; 8:33

Unit 27 (p. 111)
1. 22   2. 15
3. 16   4. 9
5. 32   6. 12
7. 18   8. 53

Unit 28 (p. 113)
1. Check students' work.
2. 2
3. 4
4. 6
5. Check students' work.
6. 2
7. 7
8. 5

Unit 28 (p. 114)
1. Check students' work.
2. 7
3. 2
4. 8
5. Check students' work.
6. 3
7. 6
8. 2

Unit 28 (p. 115)
1. Check students' work.
2. 5
3. 10
4. 5
5. Check students' work.
6. 1
7. 3
8. 2

Answer Key (Unit 29–30)

Unit 29 (p. 117)
1. 3
2. 4
3. 1
4. 8

Unit 29 (p. 118)
1. Check students' work.
2. 2
3. 5
4. 7
5. Check students' work.
6. 5
7. 35
8. 155

Unit 29 (p. 119)
1. Check students' work.
2. bologna and ham
3. 3
4. 2
5. Check students' work.
6. 50
7. 200
8. 350

Unit 30 (p. 121)
1. equally likely as
2. equally likely as
3. more likely than
4. equally likely as
5. less likely than
6. less likely than
7. equally likely as
8. less likely than
9. more likely than

Unit 30 (p. 122)
1. true   2. false
3. true   4. false
5. true   6. true
7. more likely than
8. equally likely as
9. less likely than
10. more likely than
11. less likely than
12. more likely than

Unit 30 (p. 123)
1. star
2. square; triangle
3. circle
4. true
5. C
6. B

Answer Key (STAAR Practice Test 1)

pp. 124–147

1. D
2. C
3. B
4. C
5. D
6. C
7. A
8. D
9. C
10. C
11. C
12. B
13. C
14. C
15. D
16. D
17. C
18. C
19. D
20. A
21. B
22. D
23. D
24. D
25. C
26. B
27. B
28. B
29. B
30. B
31. D
32. A
33. C
34. D
35. C
36. C
37. C
38. D
39. D
40. B
41. D
42. A
43. B
44. 24
45. 88
46. 51

Answer Key (STAAR Practice Test 2)

pp. 148–168

1. D	13. D	25. A	37. C
2. A	14. C	26. D	38. B
3. C	15. A	27. D	39. C
4. B	16. D	28. D	40. C
5. B	17. D	29. B	41. B
6. C	18. B	30. B	42. B
7. A	19. A	31. D	43. A
8. C	20. C	32. D	44. 75
9. C	21. C	33. C	45. 14
10. D	22. D	34. D	46. 07 or 7
11. B	23. A	35. A	
12. D	24. C	36. B	

STAAR Mathematics Practice Grade 3 • ©2013 Newmark Learning, LLC